"There might be no more essential in[...]
Scott talks about in this engaging bo[...]
Deception

"Wonderful book. I could hardly put it down. Thanks for bringing this powerful "story" to the world. . . .Like fish discovering water, Scott Gornto helps us all discover ourselves as unconscious storytellers swimming in stories we unknowingly make up that tend to feed our anxiety about events that have not happened, and may not happen, but thinking they are descriptions of reality. Thus we are not present to our own experience or to that of others who usually are our main characters. He does not leave us there but offers a process to move from the nightmare of our imagination to reality; a way to be present to others with curiosity and without judgment. This book is for everyone because it is about everyone." | **Harville Hendrix, Ph. D.** and **Helen Lakelly Hunt, Ph. D.** co-authors *Making Marriage Simple and Getting the Love You Want*

"Stories are central to our universal psyches. The Greeks gave us mythology, Jesus told parables, Grimm created fairytales, Lucas penned Star Wars, and Schultz composed the legacy of Charlie Brown. Leave it to Scott Gornto to bring "the stories we tell ourselves" to the human experience! Down-to-earth, insightful, contemporary, and refreshing, Scott leaves us with a practical psychological blueprint that can add meaning and health to our relationships and lives." | **Hal Barkley, Ph.D.**, LMFT-S, LPC-S, Certified Sex Therapist (AASECT) and Clinical Associate Professor and Department Chair, Dispute Resolution and Counseling at Southern Methodist University (SMU)

"What do healthy lives have to do with healthy relationships? How does our thinking and talking about each other affect our well-being? Therapist Scott Gornto shows us how storytelling shapes our lives and measures our wholeness." | **J. Randall O'Brien**, President of Carson-Newman University

"I have known Scott Gornto for 40 years. His words about being a good listener instead of making assumptions is paramount in personal and professional relationships." | **Nolan Ryan,** former Major League Baseball pitcher and chief executive officer of the Texas Rangers.

"In 'The Stories We Tell Ourselves', Scott Gornto shares the powerful ways we lie to ourselves and how those lies, which are often created in our heads, affect our feelings towards the people in our lives. This book walks us through the journey of awakening to those truths and growing beyond the stories we imagine to attain healthy, confident relationships." | **John McKinzie**, Lead Pastor, Hope Fellowship - Frisco, Texas

R. SCOTT GORNTO

THE STORIES
WE TELL
OURSELVES

STOP JUMPING TO CONCLUSIONS
FREE YOURSELF FROM ANXIETY
TRANSFORM YOUR RELATIONSHIPS

THE STORIES WE TELL OURSELVES™
Stop Jumping to Conclusions. Free Yourself from Anxiety. Transform Your Relationships.
By R. Scott Gornto
Auxano Publishing

Published by Auxano Publishing, Plano, Texas

Editor: Blake Atwood, www.editfor.me
Proofreader: Rebecca L. McCarthy, www.thewrittencoach.com
Index: Elena Gwynne, www.quillandinkindexing.com
Cover design: Micah Kandros, www.micahkandrosdesign.com
Interior design and layout: Yvonne Parks, www.PearCreative.ca
Cover copy: Tracy Carlson, www.rightbrainbrands.com
Megan E. Bryant, www.meganebryant.com

Library of Congress Control Number: 2014916056
ISBN: 978-0-9907191-0-6 (softcover)
ISBN: 978-0-9907191-1-3 (hardcover)

ATTENTION CORPORATIONS, UNIVERSITIES, COLLEGES, AND PROFESSIONAL ORGANIZATIONS: Quantity discounts are available on bulk purchases of this book for educational, gift purposes, or as premiums for increasing magazine subscriptions or renewals. Special books or book excerpts can also be created to fit specific needs. For information, please contact Auxano Publishing, 6101 Chapel Hill Blvd., Plano, TX 75093, 972.312.8893 or info@rscottgornto.com

To Crystal, Noah, and Oakley

TABLE OF CONTENTS

SECTION FOUR:
THE PRACTICE

ACKNOWLEDGMENTS

I owe a huge thank you to:

My wife Crystal, for your love, strength, honesty, grace, and support through this project and for the past twelve years. Thank you.

My boys Noah and Oakley. May you continue to be a blessing to others and bring light and life into the world.

My parents Rick and Janice, for your love, support, wisdom, selflessness, and generosity over the many years. Thank you.

Harris, Jen, Avery, Sutton, and Jude, for your love and friendship. I am grateful we are on this journey of life together.

Kyle, our hearts still ache. I am grateful that the bond of brotherhood doesn't end in death.

My team who has been a huge support to me: Angelia Cagan, Janica Smith, Elizabeth Marshall, Blake Atwood, Dennis Welch, Michelle Meals, Yvonne Parks, Rebecca L. McCarthy, Micah Kandros, Tracy Carlson, and Megan E. Bryant, Jason Mitchell, and Harris Bechtol.

My influencers: Dr. Randall O'Brien, Louie Giglio, Dr. Randy Northrup, Dr. David Augsburger, Dr. Ray Anderson, Catherine Gregg, Kathy Christopher, Wayne Albrecht, Brad Watts, Sheila Madigan-Levatino, Charles Vorkoper, Rick Carson, Lynn Grodski, Suzanne Kaufman, Hal Barkley, Susan Swank, and Rod Masteller.

And lastly, my clients past and present.

INTRODUCTION

Imagine what your life would be like with less stress and anxiety.

Imagine what your relationships would be like if they were deeper, longer lasting, and more fulfilling.

Imagine what you would be like if the best possible version of you showed up in your relationships.

If you have trouble imagining such a future, I'm thrilled that you've picked up my book. This book will help you reduce your personal anxiety, decrease loneliness, and improve your relationships. It will also teach you methods and strategies that will enhance your peace, your joy, and your fulfillment. Your life is about to change!

This book is a culmination of the past 20+ years of extensive research on relationships, human behavior, the mind, and emotions. As a licensed marriage and family therapist (LMFT), a certified sex therapist (AASECT), and an expert on relationships and personal development, I've worked with thousands of clients, ranging from teenagers to pro athletes, individuals to those in committed relationships, and company executives to pastors. I can attest to the fact that this information has helped thousands of my clients. Additionally, as a result of my research, I created the Auxano Approach© to relationships: a developmental approach to therapy that highlights how marriage and relationship(s) challenge us to grow emotionally and relationally.

Based on my research with clients as well as personal experience, our heightened states of anxiety and our lack of fulfilling relationships stem from a single origin: the stories we tell ourselves.

What are these stories? Where do they come from? Why do we tell them so often? Can we get rid of them? How much better could life be if we stopped telling ourselves these stories? What if the stories we tell ourselves are true? All of these questions and more will be answered in the pages that follow.

If our desire is to experience true, deep, and lasting connections with others in our lives, we must be willing to notice, pause, and rewrite the stories we tell ourselves.

One quick note: don't skip chapters. Much like an athlete must lift lighter weights before attempting heavier weights, so, too, must you strengthen your mental and emotional muscle memory before moving onto the next steps. Each chapter in *The Stories We Tell Ourselves* builds upon the previous chapter.

In the following pages, you will venture down a pathway to emotional and relational maturity. On this journey you'll meet

INTRODUCTION

Steve, Lauren, and Emma, a small family whose relationship problems mirror many of those I hear about from my clients. You'll also read stories with real life clients. *Names have been changed and story lines have been modified to protect my clients' privacy.* I'll share personal anecdotes as well. Even though I'm a licensed therapist, I'm also human, and that means there's still emotional and relational maturation to accomplish in my own life.

You're about to embark upon a challenging personal development journey, yet the reward at the end will be worth the effort. By the end of our time together, you'll be able to notice the stories you tell yourself, where those stories come from, and how they affect your anxiety and relationships. You will also learn strategies to reduce the internal narratives—so the don't continue to have a subconscious stronghold on your thoughts and emotions. With the stories and strategies I share, like the Auxano Approach© to communication and relationships, your anxiety can decrease. Additionally, your relationships will become more fulfilling as you develop awareness and learn the art of being present.

Now, let's meet Steve, Lauren, and Emma at a time when they should be at their most relaxed—on vacation in the Bahamas.

SECTION ONE: THE PREMISE

"I'm making up stories? Really?"

A STORY ABOUT OUR STORIES

"I wanted a perfect ending. Now I've learned, the hard way, that some poems don't rhyme, and some stories don't have a clear beginning, middle, and end." | Gilda Radner

PARADISE LOST

"We're in paradise, Steve. Can't you put your phone down for at least a few minutes and enjoy what's right in front of you?"

Setting his phone on the sand, Steve looks at his wife Lauren with a sheepish grin, a smile she knows all too well. It's the look he gives her when he's been caught being somewhere else.

"I'm sorry, hon. I just wanted to check in and see if things were okay at work. You know how it's been there."

"Of course I do. It's all you talk about lately, like it's the only important thing in your life. If you're not careful, you're going to miss the last few years we have with Emma."

Steve surveys the shoreline and spots his sixteen-year-old daughter talking with a young man too tan for his own good.

"Well, someone has to pay the bills."

"Can we not do this on our vacation?"

"You're right. I'm sorry. I won't check my phone again."

Bzzz. Bzzz. Bzzz. Bzzz.

As Steve glances at his phone, Lauren sighs.

"It's an email from Sheri. I have to at least look at it."

"Fine," Lauren replies. "I'm going for a walk. If you're not going to be here, then neither am I."

Steve picks up his phone and swipes open the email from his supervisor: *Need to talk with you when you get back.* As his body tightens and his heart begins to run laps around his mind, he realizes that Lauren was right—he definitely shouldn't have checked his email while on vacation. Wanting to know more about his current predicament, Steve taps out a quick reply: *Having fun on vacation with the family. Look forward to talking when I get back in the office. Can you give me an idea of the topic we'll be discussing? I'd like to prepare.*

He closes his phone and drops it in the sand, heaving a sigh of frustration as he closes his eyes to the paradise that surrounds him. Of all days, why did this have to happen today? As he tries to fall asleep, Steve attempts to fill in the gaps of Sheri's much too short and much too vague email.

Maybe it's a raise? Yeah, right. When's the last time that actually happened? I should have closed that sale before I left on this trip. I'm probably going to get fired. Sheri never liked me. I should have seen this coming. What will I do for work now? How will I pay the bills? Remember how hard it was on Lauren when I was out of work for three months a few years ago? How can I do this to her again? I've seen enough movies to know that it's probably just a matter of time until she leaves me for someone who can actually hold down a job.

He tosses and turns until the voices in his head finally go hoarse, leaving him in a fitful state for a nap on the beach.

Many hours later, he's startled awake by Lauren. It's dark and she's frantic.

"Why are you still here? Do you know where Emma is?"

"No idea. She's old enough to take care of herself."

"No, she's not Steve, especially not while on vacation. She told me she was going for a long walk with that boy and she'd be back here by eight. It's nine now, and she hasn't answered my texts or my calls. What if they're drinking,

9

Steve? What if they're fooling around? What if they went swimming at dusk and something terrible happened and no one could see them to help?"

"You're being ridiculous Lauren. We're not in the middle of some bad *Baywatch* episode. She probably just lost track of time. It's happened before."

On the first day of their vacation, Emma met the man she was sure she'd marry. She knew he didn't know it yet, but she was certain of it nonetheless, as sixteen-year-olds often are. She could see their future together, and possibly even their tiny, sun-kissed children. This epiphany occurred the moment she first saw him. She knew then that the rest of her vacation would be spent with one goal in mind.

On the second day of their vacation, she'd succeeded at step one: meeting him. His name was Evan, and he appeared genuinely interested in her, so much so that they even exchanged phone numbers. Much later that night, she texted him to see if he'd like to go for a walk the next day.

Twenty-four hours went by without a reply. As each hour passed, Emma's future Disney princess story unraveled. She waved goodbye to her small, blonde surfer children. She mentally tore up the simple gown she would have worn at their beachside wedding. She cried over what would have been their first date, as he would have tried in vain to teach her how to surf, but she would have had fun anyway.

Her mind adds insult to the injury her future's just sustained:

We just met. Why should I even expect a reply? Maybe he was just being nice to me earlier because there were people nearby. Maybe it's like my friends have told me and he just pretends to be a good guy so he can get girls' numbers like some sort of trophy. Or maybe he lost his phone. Oh, I bet I know what it was: I wasn't wearing makeup when we met. He probably thinks I'm an uggo.

Emma skipped dinner with her family that night. They didn't ask why. They seldom did.

Bzzz. Bzzz. Bzzz. Bzzz.

Emma bolts awake and looks at her phone. It's one in the morning, but it's a text . . . *from him!* She falls out of her bed in reaching for her phone: *Sry I didn't reply sooner. My phone bit it while I was surfing early yesterday morning. Finally got a new one. Still up for that walk?*

Emma immediately texts back: *Yes, of course. 3pm tomorrow?*

Sounds good. C U then.

Mentally, Emma begins to sew her simple gown back together.

"Where have you been young lady? You had me worried sick. Why didn't you answer your phone? Are you trying to upset me on purpose?"

"I'm sorry Mom. I lost track of time. We were just walking. Promise."

"We have just a few days left of this *family* vacation, so no more boy time for you. You've lost that privilege."

"But Mom! You can't do that to me! We just met and . . . and . . . I think he really likes me."

"Honey, just think about reality for half a moment. How are you two going to date when we go back home? Are you going to come visit him, or is he going to come visit you? Or do you just plan to text each other all the time on the phone that you apparently don't know how to use?"

Emma begins to sob quietly.

Steve finally interjects, "C'mon Lauren, that's unfair. You're being harsh."

"Well, someone needs to be. Lord knows you've been elsewhere on this trip too. Why did we even come on a *family* vacation if everyone wants to be somewhere else?"

Lauren's cutting question hangs in the air. All three family members know she's just spoken the truth, but none of them want to face it. Without another word, they return to their rooms and start packing for their long flight back home the next day.

On the Monday following their failed vacation, Steve slowly walks into Sheri's office.

"For a guy that's been in the Caribbean for a week, you look like you need a vacation from your vacation. Everything alright?"

"It was a good vacation," Steve lies. "Just a little worn out now, I guess . . . What did you want to see me about? I was kind of wondering about it most of the week."

"I'm sorry about that. My husband and I took a last-minute vacation too, up to our lake house. It's great for getting away from it all, but terrible for cell phone reception. I hope you weren't worried by my email."

"No. Of course not," Steve lies again. "Just curious."

"No need to be worried. I'll cut to the chase so we can both get back to work. I spoke with my manager early last week. You've been doing well here—even though you probably think we don't notice these things—and we'd like to offer you a promotion."

Steve laughs.

"So you really were worried about that email I sent?"

"Yeah. A bit. To be honest, I didn't expect a promotion."

"Well, you should tell yourself better stories."

WHO ARE YOU?

In the story you just read, who are you? Are you Steve, fearful of what may come your way at work on any given week? Or are you Lauren, envisioning every possible negative outcome from your teenager's expanding freedom? Or are you Emma, a romantic who paints a lush future with only the barest of materials to begin?

Even if you don't immediately identify with any of these fictional characters, you've likely written fanciful stories in your own mind about future experiences, and these made-up stories likely ended with negative consequences. You may have hoped for a positive result in a given situation, but a louder voice in your head shouted that possibility away, leaving you with a hollow feeling that a bad experience is more than likely waiting for you around the next bend. Take a moment right now and recall a recent incident where you may have told yourself such a story.

Did that story resolve like you thought it would? Or, was your fiction trumped by truth? In fact, how often was the simplest explanation of an event the actual explanation of that event, like Evan losing his phone in the opening story?

Once you start noticing the stories you fabricate on a daily basis and compare those outcomes to what actually happens in reality, you'll begin to see that a wide chasm exists between the two. Our relationships fall into this chasm when we relate to other people based on our made-up stories rather than reality. It's these stories we tell ourselves that ultimately prevent us from relating to others in a healthy way. When we can begin to listen to our internal monologue and identify the irrationality of the stories we create, we can then become much more proactive about the way these stories affect, *and infect*, our relationships. In time, learning to differentiate between the fiction of our minds and the truth of our relationships will lead to less anxiety and more peace, less worry and more trust, fewer broken relationships and more healthy bonds.

> **Once you start noticing the stories you fabricate on a daily basis and compare those outcomes to what actually happens in reality, you'll begin to see that a wide chasm exists between the two.**

Unfortunately, you can't just flip a switch in your mind to shut off that internal chatterbox. (*If you can, please let me know.*) Like an athlete, you have to train yourself every day to do this. Essentially, you have to work the muscles of your mind as consistently as a trained athlete exercises. As time progresses, your mental muscle memory will increase, allowing you to be fully present with someone so that you can engage the actual person across from you instead of the "fantastical" person you've created them to be. Like physical training, this requires particular strategies, which we'll get to later in the book.

For now, let's dive back in to Steve, Lauren, and Emma's story.

YOU'RE THE STAR

Did you catch the common theme in the opening story?

Confronted by a problem they didn't want to face, each character filled in the blanks and drew their own wild conclusions about their particular situation. Steve received a short, vague email from his boss and automatically assumed the worst. Despite knowing her mostly well-behaved daughter for sixteen years, Lauren fears the worst when Emma doesn't return at a set time. Wide-eyed, in-love Emma dreams large. Consequently, her reality presents a jarring, unwelcome contrast. Each character had scant information to begin with, but that didn't prevent each of them from building an entire world of inevitable, negative possibilities.

IT'S LIKE PLAYING MAD LIBS WITH REALITY:

- (PERSON) just told me (PHRASE) about my (PROFESSION), and that must mean I'm (ADJECTIVE).

- (PERSON #1) said (PHRASE) to (PERSON #2) about me, which means (PERSON #1) is (ADJECTIVE).

- My (HUSBAND/WIFE) just said (PHRASE), so that probably means we're (ADJECTIVE).

But maybe word games aren't your thing, so here's another metaphor for this constant battle between truth and our interpretation of reality that our Netflix-bingeing culture can relate to: movies.

When you write stories in your head, you're the screenwriter, director, and star of your own major motion picture. You cast yourself as the hero—even if the hero suffers greatly at the beginning—and you cast everyone else as secondary characters, many to whom you'd rather not award speaking parts. Maybe your spouse gets to play a supporting character, but that's about it. You are the Brad Pitt or Angelina Jolie of your mind, the one around whom the world revolves, the one who demands attention simply because you're there.

> **When you write stories in your head, you're the screenwriter, director, and star of your own major motion picture.**

In your stories, everyone else reacts to you, the star, and they react *in just the way you imagine because you wrote the script!* There's no free-will deviation from the plot because the characters in your movie say the lines that you imagine them to say at the time you want them to say it. Your actors are the most compliant group of artists you've ever met. This is a fantasy world that real life directors would love, but it's a world we often inhabit within our minds. We script movies for other people, then we're shocked when they don't read the right lines or act the way we imagined.

The thing is, we all do this. We are all the main characters of our own stories, interacting with caricatures of others in the theater of our minds. So what happens when all of these protagonists meet in real life, with each person starring in their own film and failing to relate to the real people around them?

Relational chaos. Anxiety. Fear. Distrust. Anger. Frustration. Confusion. Hurt.

Much of the pain in relationships can be traced back to the stories we tell ourselves. Through unique strategies I'll provide throughout this book, like learning to be truly present, we can become more relationally aware, adept, and whole.

> **Much of the pain in relationships can be traced back to the stories we tell ourselves.**

THE STORY I'M TELLING YOU

"Promoted Steve," "learning-to-trust Lauren," and "still-in-love Emma" illustrate the main points of *The Stories We Tell Ourselves*:

- **We prefer fiction to fact** because fiction is much easier to deal with than real life. Adjusting ourselves to the facts, or learning to live with uncertainty wh3en we don't have enough information, is much harder and less satisfying.

- **We are compelled by our own stories** because they come from powerful places within us. They give voice to our hopes and fears, prejudices and preferences, as well as our values and most intimate experiences.

- **We must learn to be present** in order to genuinely engage with real people in the real world. That means listening, sharing, and investing ourselves in moments with them. In turn, such presence will silence our precious stories, which can be painful as well as liberating.

- **We will always fight this battle.** It's unlikely that we'll be able to completely abandon our imagined stories at all times. (In fact, sometimes our imagined stories *are the right stories*, an issue I'll cover later.) However, we can learn strategies for engaging with and embracing real people as they actually exist in the real world.

So what's a born storyteller supposed to do? If we're all so good at fabricating fictions and seldom noticing it when we do, how can we take steps toward a healthy inner monologue that seeks to truly understand another person on their terms and not based on our own pre-written script?

Well, it's a choice you must make on a consistent basis.

You can continue to be driven more by your imagination than seeking to truly engage others. You can continue to make up stories to fill in the blanks of a future situation. You can continue to process what happens around you as scenes in your own Oscar-worthy movie.

But if you continue doing so, your relationships will suffer from misunderstanding, misjudgments, mistakes, and missed opportunities. You will find other people's actions confusing because you aren't considering them as independent identities. You will keep on making mistakes with your spouse, family, neighbors, and coworkers. You will repeatedly miss opportunities to genuinely know other people or allow them to really know you. All of these unfortunate situations can occur because of the power of your imagination and the stories you tell yourself on a constant basis.

We exchange truth for powerful lies, and while we fiddle with fantasies, real life passes by.

So let's do the opposite. Let's reveal the lies of our own stories and insist on powerful truth.

Turn off the movies in your mind. Lay down your scripts for other people. Stop the constant thinking about your own needs when you're with someone else. Learn to look at them, to truly listen to them. Discover what it means to be present, even when the cacophony of life threatens to overtake you. Admit to not knowing everything. Be patient and humble while you wait and learn. Choose to pay attention to what's going on around you. Engage with the here and now.

> **Turn off the movies in your mind.**

The journey you're about to embark upon won't be easy. Like a heavy backpack weighing you down, you'll have to lay aside your compelling, self-serving narratives in order to reach the end of this trail. Stripped of this baggage, you may discover truths about yourself—and others—that will make you uncomfortable, but these truths will ultimately set you free. They will also lead you into relational health with your spouse, your children, your parents, your friends, and even that strange guy at work with whom you seldom want to talk.

To press pause on the false stories we tell ourselves is to arrive at a place where we're living an abundant life, a life characterized by living awake—aware and open to the grand possibilities real life—and real people—present to us.

So, let's get going.

REAL LIFE VS. REEL LIFE

"Our life is what our thoughts make it." | Marcus Aurelius

REAL LIFE STORIES

It's easy to make a compelling argument for a thesis when that argument consists of a fictional story, like the opening narrative about Steve, Lauren, and Emma on a vacation that went awry because of the many different stories they told themselves about other people. Because I'm creating that story, I can turn it to support my argument that the stories we tell ourselves are a fundamental, problematic issue at the root of our relationships. Because they're "reel people" playing parts in the "movie" of my book, I can ensure that they're all talking past each other and living in their heads instead of living in the moment.

Yet, moments in their respective stories may have resonated with you. Suddenly these "reel people" become "real people" to you, whether you may have seen yourself as Lauren, Steve, or Emma, or you spied someone you care for in one of those characters. From Steve's anxiety about his job to Lauren's concern for her daughter to Emma's desire for a romantic relationship, most people can relate to such issues. Why is that? Because the stories within that story are based in reality. How do I know this?

For the last fifteen years, I have worked as a therapist, coach, and guide to thousands of clients. In my daily work, I strive to help people establish genuine, meaningful, life-giving connections with each other. That's one of the reasons this book exists. My perspective on psychotherapy takes into account the biological, psychological, social, and spiritual issues that form a holistic and complete view of the person. By working to understand the many motivations that cause people to speak, think, and act the way they do, my goal is to help each and every client understand themselves better so that they can be proactive in establishing healthy connections with other people.

During the first few years of my practice, I noticed a subtle thread weaving its way through most every client's story. When their relationships were on shaky ground—whether it was their marriage, dating life, parenting, friendships, or business relationships—the stories they told themselves about other people increased their own anxiety and severely lessened their chances at truly connecting with that person. In other words, my clients would so often live in their heads, talking to self-fabricated versions of real life people. Before assessing the situation, they had already determined how to approach that person based on the stories they had made up, rather than based on reality. You read how this happens in the opening chapter, but I now want to share with you five different real life client stories from my practice. *Names have been changed and elements of each story have been modified to protect my clients' privacy.* While these stories are vastly dissimilar, you'll notice just as I did that a common thread runs through them all.

THE $300,000 MISTAKE

Paul and Candace, both in their late thirties, had been married for ten years. They had well-paying jobs, but Paul was still nervous about supporting their current lifestyle well into their future. Consequently, on the advice of a trusted friend, Paul invested their entire life savings—all $300,000 of it—into an overseas account. He was assured that the investment would double within a decade and could do even better over the long haul. A month after transferring the money, Paul received an email from his friend: they'd both been fleeced by a scam. While Paul scrambled to find some kind of recourse to recoup his money, his mind kept focusing on what his wife would think when she found out what he had done with their life savings. Even the thought of talking to her about it made his anxiety rise. So Paul tried to avoid every financial conversation he could with Candace.

The story Paul told himself during this time is that if he told Candace the truth about what he had done, she would be disappointed in him, wouldn't be able to handle the problem, or, worst of all, would divorce him. He couldn't bear the thought of any of those possibilities, so he tried to hide his actions from her for as long as possible. However, Candace knew something was amiss with their finances, and she waited as long as she could so that Paul might share what happened when he was ready. Eventually, she confronted him with what she knew, and it was close enough to the truth that Paul finally relented and shared what had really happened. Much to his surprise, Candace did not leave him. It certainly was painful news for Candace to digest, but they both wanted to work through it together. After some hard discussions in therapy, Paul's remorse combined with Candace's acceptance of Paul—showing him love and grace—increased their closeness and resilience as a couple. It was an outcome he never expected, a story he never told himself.

THE ABSENT ALCOHOLIC

Luke and Leah had been married for fifteen years. Early on, Luke would ease his anxiety about his job and his new marriage by escaping into alcohol abuse. Unsettling events involving Luke's alcohol abuse would seem to occur every three months. He would call Leah to say that he was going to be late to dinner because he was going to "grab a few with the boys" before heading home. On these particular nights, he would arrive home after midnight horribly drunk. Leah would have called him several times, but he'd never answer. She let the issue go the first time, but as it became a habit, she sought help. She couldn't stand the fact that he drank so much and he didn't seem to care if she was frantic about when—or if—he'd be home after these binges.

Luke went through a year of therapy and joined a support group. He learned why he was drawn to drinking, and he enjoyed success against his alcoholism . . . for a time. Eventually, he began to drink at home some, just a beer or a glass of wine every few days. One day in particular, Luke was headed home from work and called Leah to say that he needed to stop by a friend's house "real quick" to pick up some tools. After an hour and a half elapsed with no word from and no sign of Luke, Leah's mind goes back to the place it knows so well: Luke's out drinking again.

Because of their history, Leah filled in the blanks of her situation and told herself the story that Luke must definitely be out drinking with his buddies again. To her, it was the only logical conclusion. She texted him and said, *"Here we go again, you're avoiding me and you're drinking again, aren't you?"* A few minutes after she sent the text, Luke got home, fuming. She could tell that he wasn't drunk, but she was also just as angry as him. He told her that he'd just gotten to talking with his friend whom he hadn't seen in awhile and lost track of time, then he related how upset it made him that she thought he was out drinking again, especially after all of the hard work he had done over the last year. Leah asked him to consider his story from her perspective and his history. He agreed that he could understand why she would think that, but he also reinforced how much actual progress he'd made in the last year.

FLIRTATION OR FRIENDSHIP?

Susan was in her early forties and had been dating fifty-year-old Mike for two years. Neither of them had been married before. Mike was outgoing and personable, two qualities that initially attracted Susan. However, as their relationship progressed, she learned that he had many female friends. Each time she learned that Mike was meeting up with one of his female friends, she would become instantly anxious and assume that he was flirting with her and wanted out of their relationship. She would write story after story in her mind about the way Mike and a female friend would spend their time together, often going to extremes in terms of what they were likely doing together. Over time, those unfounded opinions cemented themselves into a hardened belief system about Mike. She began to believe that Mike was flirting with his female friends, talking negatively about Susan to these women, and using these women in order get needs met that he wasn't getting met in their relationship, whether sexual, emotional, or both. Consequently, Mike and Susan's relationship began to erode quickly as Susan was constantly anxious and judgmental while Mike withdrew from her constant scrutiny.

When Susan and Mike met with me, I helped Susan see how her unfounded beliefs had created a wall of safety around her. Because she was so enamored with Mike and had been hurt multiple times in the past from cheating boyfriends and a dad who had left her at an early age, she had subconsciously erected a wall in order to protect herself from getting hurt again. While such a wall might protect a person's feelings, it also keeps other people out. She had built a protective barrier that was also a defense mechanism, and every time she chose to believe the false stories she told herself about Mike, she was preventing the one person she most loved from drawing near to her. With these beliefs that she had developed such a staunch loyalty to over time, she hadn't left any room for the relationship to breathe. Even though Susan thought she was doing her due diligence in keeping tabs on Mike, she was stifling the relationship.

Eventually, Mike said, "I can't compete with your belief system." What he meant is that he couldn't compete with the version of himself that Susan had already created in her mind. She was so sure that he was cheating on her in some way that even his best protestations of the fact fell on deaf ears. After Mike agreed to a lie detector test (at Susan's prodding) with hopes to calm her fears, the results came back that Mike wasn't flirting and employed healthy and respectful boundaries with his female friends. But Susan couldn't see that, or chose not to. Their relationship failed, in part because Susan's belief system was stronger than the relationship itself.

MOM VS. DAD

David was a fourteen-year-old eighth grader placed in the toughest of positions. His parents had recently divorced, and his mom wanted to ensure that David chose her side in the battle. Consequently, she conducted subversive, covert parent alienation. In other words, she would bad-mouth David's father to David in an effort to turn him against his father. As an impressionable teen desiring to please his mom, David convinced himself that his dad didn't love him or care for him. In addition to the stresses of daily life in junior high, David had to cope with the constant stress of his home life, but he didn't know how to do so. He acted out and sometimes showcased a violent temper.

The father, wanting to seek a healthy relationship with his son, talked with me. Eventually, I spoke with both the father and the son in the same room. David's father revealed that he does, in fact, care deeply for his son. A breakthrough in their relationship occurred when David recognized that and saw it to be true. When I asked if David had ever considered directly asking his father the many questions that he had already made up answers for in his mind, David shook his head from side to side and said, "How could I? I was so angry with him. I didn't want anything to do with him. But I guess I should have gotten both sides of the story."

Over time, David and I worked on self-calming techniques, strategies that he could use when he felt his temper beginning to flare. He learned that all we can control is our own skin and experience, and that enjoying life is impossible when your mind makes up false stories that only make you miserable on the inside. Even though we helped to resolve the false story David had concocted about his dad, we still had further work to do because David was now concocting false stories about his mom on account of the fact that she had lied to him about his dad. In each case though, David was learning how to differentiate the incomplete stories in his mind from the truth of his present circumstances.

GOD OF JUDGMENT

Elizabeth was a married woman in her mid-fifties, and both of her kids were in college. With less busyness in her life to distract her from hard, internal realities, she began struggling with depression. She kept telling herself that God was somehow judging her for certain poor decisions she'd made during her life. She was a mostly quiet person, but her deepening depression caused even more withdrawal from her relationships. She did little to fix it as she believed she was "less than" everybody else in her life. It was a vicious cycle as well, because she assumed her depression was part of God's judgment of her.

Through our sessions together, we eventually discovered one of the triggering factors in Elizabeth's feelings of inadequacy. While a child and a teenager, her father always acted in a "one-up" manner, constantly berating Elizabeth and letting her know that she never quite measured up to his expectations. When she would try to speak her own mind, he would casually dismiss her, sometimes even to the point of being verbally abusive. Over time, she grew weary of trying to persuade him differently. So she learned to play the part of the voiceless, submissive daughter. Just beneath the surface of her facade, she began to resent her father and silently counted the days until she could go off to college. From an early age, she began telling herself the story that what she said and did were inconsequential—that she didn't really matter to anyone.

Elizabeth's troubling relationship with her father is a family of origin problem, something we'll discuss in detail in Chapter 6, and an issue that many of my clients struggle with, even well into their older years. In talking with Elizabeth, I relayed that anytime we squelch our emotions, opinions, or feelings about something, they will find a way to escape, like rainwater running toward a river. In such instances, we will either "act out" or "act in." Acting out can occur through easily seen issues like addictions, compulsive behavior, or escapism. On the other hand, acting in can sometimes be more difficult to assess because it manifests as depression or anxiety.

Because of Elizabeth's faith, her internal moral compass would not allow her to act out because she feared being judged by God for wanting to do specific things or even thinking particular thoughts, especially when it came to her dad. Consequently, she subconsciously "acted in" and became depressed. Through our work together, she came to see God in a different light, one not so shadowed by her father's immense presence in her internal world. Through guided imagery, talk therapy, and helpful books, Elizabeth arrived at a place of self-belief and self-confidence through telling herself a new narrative about herself as well as how God saw her. She began telling herself that she did, in fact, matter, and even more so, that she mattered greatly to God. In time, her depression lifted.

THE THREAD WITHIN THESE CLIENT STORIES

We are master storytellers, especially when it comes to our relationships. This can cause our relationships to be discouraging, anxiety-laden, fearful, stressful, and challenging. As these real life client stories attest, the stories we tell ourselves affect all types of relationships in many different ways. Additionally, our stories often reveal themselves to be false in time. While there are certainly instances where such stories are true, an issue I'll discuss in a later chapter, many of the stories we tell ourselves are fabrications woven together with little more than the barest of threads and the smallest of needles.

> **Many of the stories we tell ourselves are fabrications woven together with little more than the barest of threads and the smallest of needles.**

We craft these stories based on the scripts we pick up throughout our lives. These internal scripts can stem from our family of origin, our past hurts, pop culture, and a wide array of other story-laden sources, and we'll look at each of these sources in depth in future chapters. When we choose to believe our own fabricated stories over the truth of reality as it presents itself to us, we give way to heightened anxiety and shallow relationships. This book seeks to help you reverse this natural trend to tell yourself stories so that you might be able to pause the stories you tell yourself in order for your anxiety to lessen and your relationships to deepen.

> **We craft these stories based on the scripts we pick up throughout our lives.**

Now, let's see how the stories Lauren tells herself about Steve ultimately work to heighten her anxiety and place stress on their relationship.

WHEN STORIES RUSH IN

"Your assumptions are your windows on the world. Scrub them off every once in a while, or the light won't come in." | Isaac Asimov

THE OTHER WOMAN

"Am I being ridiculous? Should I be worried about Steve? Would he really leave me for someone else?"

Jamie pauses before responding to Lauren, a telling sign that causes Lauren to sigh deeply.

"Jamie, your silence might as well have been a blatant yes. You're my friend. You're supposed to help me combat my worries."

"I wasn't silent because I think it could be true. I was honestly considering the question in light of what you told me. I know you don't want to do this, but let's run through the list again: emotionally unavailable, disinterested in casual conversation with you, and little to no advances in the bedroom."

"Check, check, and unfortunately, check."

"His company just hired a new, young blonde who you've heard is gorgeous."

"I've seen her. She is. No way I can compete."

"Don't say that about yourself. You offer so much more, from your looks to your brains to your caring and kindness. Don't talk down to yourself right now. I know this is hard, but you have to try to maintain some kind of objectivity with this predicament until the truth reveals itself. You can't go jumping to conclusions based on what you know right now."

"You haven't finished the checklist. You forgot to add that he's been working more late nights, he's made a few strange cash withdrawals, *and* he's currently on a week-long business trip . . . *with her.*"

"And a dozen other people from his company. Do you think something would really go on with so many of his coworkers there?"

"I, I guess not. I really don't want to think about it. I don't know what to think about it. Doesn't it sound exactly like what happened to Susan last year? All I know is that I'm afraid he's going to come home on Saturday, pack his bags, and tell me he wants a divorce. I'm scared,

Jamie. For the first time in our seven years of marriage, I'm truly scared."

Lauren starts crying, unable to contain her emotions any longer. Her sorrow quickly turns to anger, and her anger turns on Jamie.

"You tell me Jamie: how can I be objective about something so close to me, and something that, by every show I've ever watched on TV, looks exactly like he's having an affair?"

WHAT WOULD YOU DO?

If you were Lauren, how would you confront Steve upon his return? Would you confront him at all? Would you try to tease further information from him and attempt to discover his possible lies? Or would you give him the benefit of the doubt and choose to believe that some other, less dire explanation is more likely? Either way, Lauren's in a tough situation with no easy answers and no step-by-step guide to see her through to a positive outcome.

In similar situations, many of us would follow a predictable sequence of internal storytelling, much like what Lauren relayed to her friend Jamie:

- **We would consider what we've observed or heard** and cycle the "facts" through our minds like clues to a mystery.

- **We would feel some form of increased anxiety** about what we don't know, suspecting that certain missing clues would explain the situation.

- **We would speculate about that missing information** and fill in the gaps with our best guesses and assumptions.

- **We would form semi-plausible theories** from those guesses.

- **We would settle on the theory** that best fits our bigger narrative, the greater story we believe about ourselves and our place in the world.

- **We would reorganize the information** into a coherent and compelling story, assigning roles to others that support our narrative.

Consequently, Steve must be having an affair. According to Lauren, there's no other as-likely explanation for his aberrant decisions lately. In her mind, X+Y+Z = affair, but she fails to take into account the hundreds of other variables at play in her husband's life. She attempts to connect the dots of her husband's spotty narrative to create a plausible picture, even though the image is one that would devastate her.

WHERE STORIES RUSH IN

It's not that all of our stories are bad, although they often manifest themselves that way. It's more that our stories tend to take a cue from physics in that nature hates a vacuum.

Like air rushing in when opening a new bottle of soda, our minds rush in to fill the voids of our experiences. Whether conscious of it or not, our minds despise missing information. Almost like a law of nature, we can't help ourselves. Consider history: We once thought the world was flat as well as the center of the universe (a telling sign of our hubris, for sure). These "facts" were based on what could be deduced at the time, but the men of that age still made a cosmic leap from what they could understand to what they assumed to be true. We could go even further back in history and consider ancient myth. The Greeks couldn't explain where thunder and lightning came from, so they told stories about Zeus to fill the vacuum in their understanding. The Vikings told stories of Thor and his hammer to explain the same phenomenon.

In all instances, we created stories that helped to support the world as we knew it . . . or the world as we wanted it to be. **We're wired to try to make sense of our lives based on the evidence we're provided, and if that evidence is found lacking, we become our own Sherlock Holmes and deduce a likely outcome, even with scant information.**

As in the sequence of internal storytelling outlined above, we attempt to amass as much information as we can about a situation, but once that information reaches its peak, we strive to complete the picture by relying on a number of other stories. For instance, Lauren made two telling remarks to her friend Jamie. She said that her experience sounded exactly like what their mutual friend Susan had endured and references "every show I've ever watched on TV." Lauren filled in the gaps of her story with the narratives of her friends and what she'd seen on television. Such stories can stem from a wide variety of places and experiences, like your past hurts and traumas, your parents, your peers, culture at large, movies and TV, and even your spirituality. As this book progresses, we'll dive deeper into precisely how each of these issues infiltrate and shape the stories we tell ourselves.

When we can't explain what's happening around us, especially if it affects us personally, we feel anxious. As the number of swirling unknowns increase in a given situation, it's likely that your anxiety increases as well. Such anxiety originates from a number of places, but at the beginning it mostly seems to come from the recognition of our own ignorance of the situation. That ignorance—the fact that we don't have all the facts—then causes our imagination to run wild and fill in the answers we so desperately want to know.

Pause here and consider a recent incident in your life when this held true.

Ask yourself these questions about that situation:

- **When you first learned about the situation,** what did you assume to be true?

- **When you learned the truth about the situation,** what parts of your initial story turned out to be false?

- **In between the time you assumed the truth and learned the actual truth,** how did you treat the other person in this scenario?

- **With the help of time and hindsight,** what external stories (past hurts, your family, TV, etc.) may have filled the void of your initial story?

For those of you whose eyes are being opened to the ways stories significantly affect our lives, this may be a challenging series of questions. If you have difficulty thinking of a recent scenario, finish this book and then come back to this section. These are important questions to ask yourself when looking back upon a troubling situation. In fact, these are questions you can learn to ask yourself *even in the midst of troubling situations.* Knowing how you use the stories you tell yourself is one of the key factors in learning how to proactively fight against the negative ways that our stories affect our relationships. But, again, we'll get to that.

At the moment, let's see how Lauren confronts Steve.

THE OTHER EXPLANATION

Steve steps through his front door and grandly proclaims, in his best Desi Arnaz impersonation, "Honey, I'm home!" Though weary from his weeklong business trip, he's genuinely happy to be there. He waits in the entryway for his family to come greet him, but after a few awkward, silent minutes, he walks to the kitchen.

"I've gotta go, Jamie. Steve just got home."

Lauren puts the phone down and looks at Steve. He can tell something's wrong, but he doesn't have the energy to ask, so he pulls out his go-to line for talking, but not for real conversation.

"Hi hon. How's business?"

"I should be asking you that."

"What's that supposed to mean?" His words hold venom he doesn't mean to spit. He thinks, *Where did that come from?* about both Lauren's leading accusation and his own terse reply. *I just got home!*

"I'm sorry, Steve. That came out wrong. It's been a long week with you gone is all."

"Is that really all?"

His short question hangs between them for an eternity.

Lauren tries to be stoic, but he knows her and sees her eyes beginning to tear up.

"Please tell me what's wrong, Lauren."

"Are you planning on leaving me?"

Steve's eyes widen, a genuine look of shock crossing his face.

"Why would I ever do an idiotic thing like that? I know we've had some issues lately, but it's nothing we can't work through. Why do you think I want out?"

"Because all the facts lead me to that conclusion."

"What facts?"

"When's the last time we had a conversation as long as this one? When's the last time we were intimate? Why have you had to work so late the last month? And there's that new girl at your office, and you just went on a weeklong trip for your company, and . . . you're leaving me, aren't you?"

As a light bulb of understanding pops on in Steve's mind, a sympathetic smile crosses his face.

"Honey, I'm so sorry. That's not the truth at all. I can see how you could get there, but let me be clear: I am in no way having an affair. To do so would be to give up on my best friend and our future children, and I couldn't betray you or them in that way. I do, however, confess to working too much. You remember that new client I brought in a few months back? Turns out they're very demanding, and my manager said if I could keep that client happy for at least a year, I'll be a shoo-in for a pretty good promotion next year. I'm sorry that I didn't tell you about all of that, and I apologize for not talking with you as often as I should. All of this work has made me tired for too long, but that's a poor excuse for not working on the one relationship that means more to me than anything—or anyone—else."

"Is that the truth?"

Steve raises his right hand. "God's honest. If you need proof, I can get you proof. You can watch hours and hours of security footage of me sitting at my desk. Or you can ask Bob about the trip. We roomed together and he knows I was on my laptop in the room when we weren't in meetings."

"I don't need proof Steve. I trust you. But I need you to really talk with me more often so I don't start thinking these things."

TALKING TO SOMEONE WHO DOESN'T EXIST

Lauren's response is a prime example of talking to someone who's not there. It's not that Steve isn't physically present; it's that Lauren begins her conversation by talking to the Steve she's created in her mind. She's speaking to the Steve she's written into her own script, one whose cavalier attitude toward their marriage has undoubtedly led him astray. Based off of her friend's past experience and the narratives she fills her mind with from television, she's cast herself as the victim-in-waiting, an innocent soul who's being taken advantage of by a husband who's no longer interested in her. By casting Steve in such a negative light based on her cobbled together "facts," Lauren confronts a man who doesn't exist.

> **Assumptions wreak havoc in our relationships.**

While the particular circumstances of this story may not strike a chord with you, you can likely recall a time when you were in Lauren's place and unjustly confronted someone else based on your pre-written narrative of their life. **Although such assumptions can wreak havoc in our relationships, this does not make you a "bad" person; it makes you human.** We hate being ignorant—not stupid, but ignorant—which just means we don't know something.

Anxiety and ignorance are vacuums, and our imagination rushes in to fill the space. We construct explanations. And, because it's part of human nature to organize information into narratives, our imagination writes these stories, oftentimes without our notice.

Stories are powerful organizing principles in the human mind. Generally, we don't think in terms of logical or scientific propositions. More often, we squeeze our facts and guesses into a narrative rather than constructing the story around actual data. We recognize when others cram facts into their stories, but seldom do we catch ourselves in the same act.

> **Anxiety and ignorance are vacuums, and our imagination rushes in to fill the space.**

Our imagination is so quick to tell us these stories that they happen in real time. Consequently, we talk past each other. We don't really listen to each other, we don't really understand each other, and we don't react to the actual situation at hand. Our responses are not always appropriate. We miss opportunities for engagement and growth, and we fail to solve the actual problems in front of us because we're working on imaginary problems from our inner script.

So how do we talk to someone who actually exists?

THREE WAYS TO GAUGE OUR STORIES

We may not be able to change human nature, but we can pay attention to three "dials" on the dashboard of our mind. If we monitor these, we can measure the likelihood for inappropriate storytelling and perhaps cut it off or minimize its impact on the situation.

- **The Anxiety Gauge**

  We feel anxious when we don't know enough about something that affects us. In fact, our anxiety is directly proportional to our degree of ignorance and its potential effect on our lives. **The more important something is and the less we know about it, the higher the anxiety gauge climbs.** So, like a pilot, we should carefully watch that dial. When anxiety increases, we should be on alert that our imagination may kick in as well. The more we can bring our anxiety level down (by a variety of methods we'll discuss in the chapters ahead), the less likely it is that made-up stories will rush in to fill the void in an effort to protect us from unwanted circumstances.

- **The Fact Gauge**

  Sometimes we think we know things that are actually just speculative guesses. We believe so strongly that our "facts" are truth, but it's still a belief without firm grounding in reality. The fact gauge is sensitive and can be subject to false positive readings. Accordingly, this particular gauge ought to be calibrated regularly, and we also need to learn how to read it correctly.

  Think of it less as a thermometer, which gives you a number that's easy to understand—86 degrees is 86 degrees wherever you are—and more as a barometer, which provides a number that needs additional context to understand, like one's location, temperature, and dew point, or if the number has been rising or falling over the last hour. The fact gauge helps you assess the difference between what you think and what you know. When what you know drops below fifty percent

44

in a given situation, caution is warranted. You've slipped into the speculation zone.

▪ The Presence Gauge

When you're talking to another person, do you offer them the gift of your presence? Are you listening to their actual words, or are you zoning out, making guesses, filling in the blanks for them, and planning what you're going to say next? Are you making eye contact? Are you aware of the room around you, the time, the other people there, and the details of the situation?

When your mind pulls back from the place you're in and the people you're with, your imagination then has space to fill that void, and it will fill it with a story that's more interesting and more compelling than the truth. *Your fantastic fabrication is attractive, but it lacks substance and can lead to ruined relationships.* By being aware of your levels of presence, you can begin to assess how much you're actually engaging with the other person as opposed to how much you're engaging with the story you've already written for the other person. Anyone can learn to be present, and later on, we'll cover particular strategies you can use to consistently offer the gift of your presence to others.

WHERE DO WE GO FROM HERE?

Nature hates a vacuum, and we hate not knowing as much as we can about a troubling situation. The irony is that when we fill the void with our imagination and cast ourselves and others in private dramas, we only deepen our ignorance about the issue at hand. The more we lose ourselves in our self-authored fables built on our hopes and fears, the more we make life into a movie about us with everyone else reduced to supporting roles.

Like Alice slipping through the Looking-Glass, we lose our ability to distinguish between fact and fiction. We fail to see or hear what's really going on because our compelling narrative overwhelms our senses. Our thoughts become detached and our words and actions become disconnected from those around us. As we slip into an unreal world, we become less real ourselves. So where do we pick up these scripts we seem to use every day?

ALL TOGETHER, ALL ALONE

"She lives in a world of her own—a world of—little glass ornaments..." | Tennessee Williams, *The Glass Menagerie*

ALONE IN A CROWDED ROOM

We are inundated with stories every day of our lives. Consequently, there's no end to the pre-written scripts we can try to cram into our already overstuffed mental filing cabinets. When a troubling or exciting experience happens that we're not quite sure how to deal with, we rifle through the tabs in these folders to locate the best way to react: Anger, Attraction, Confusion, Frustration, Happiness, Sorrow, etc. Each folder spills over with readily available scripts, many of which are yellow with age and covered in our fingerprints because they're the scripts we retrieve over and over again. Those are the stories we know so well that we ardently believe they hold the answers for a particular situation.

> **There's no end to the pre-written scripts we can try to cram into our already overstuffed mental filing cabinets.**

But using these scripts on a consistent basis with those around us can lead to relational ruin.

The movies in our heads isolate us. Because we cast other people as characters in our inner dramas, we struggle to truly know, engage, and enjoy them. We have a difficult time hearing what they say because we filter their words through the backstories, plots, and motivations we've already written for them, oftentimes filling in the blanks of their stories with our own imaginative flights of fancy. Such stories we tell ourselves disconnect and distract us from reality. We may be with people, but actually showing up and being emotionally and mentally present becomes almost impossible. When we live in our head and not in the here and now, it also makes it difficult for others to really know us, resulting in isolation and loneliness. Consequently, we may experience problems in our relationships or career, and our mental and moral health may likewise suffer.

> **When we live in our head and not in the here and now, it makes it difficult for others to really know us.**

As human beings, we were designed be in relationships—not just to be part of a relationship, but to really connect with one another. Connection means making the intentional choice to show up both emotionally and mentally in relationships. Practically speaking, when you are in someone else's presence, you intentionally choose to make eye contact, position your body to face toward the other person, and pay attention to where your mind goes, even (and especially) when the other person is talking. When your mind inevitably wanders off to other thoughts—how you will respond, what you need to do after the conversation, or reliving the past for a moment—you actively redirect yourself to really listen, learn, and be present with the other person. If that sounds challenging, it can be, but such active redirection is a strategy you can learn to implement on a consistent basis with the tips provided in later chapters.

> **As human beings, we were designed be in relationships.**

At the moment, let's consider how the circumstances of our lives and the environment we grew up in—two vast repositories of the stories we tell ourselves—affect the ways we seek to connect with others

LONELINESS KILLS

The 1995 film *Murder in the First* depicts our deep need for connection. Kevin Bacon plays seventeen-year-old orphan Henri Young, a soft-spoken, kind soul who's sent to a federal prison after stealing five dollars from a grocery store that doubles as a U.S. Post Office. His sister is sent to an orphanage while Henri is shuffled

THE STORIES WE TELL OURSELVES

through prisons until he's sentenced to the most notorious prison of them all: Alcatraz. He attempts a vain escape in order to find his sister and is consequently sentenced to three years and two months of solitary confinement in "the hole," as well as crippling physical abuse from the Assistant Warden. Without light, heat, a toilet, or contact with others, Henri loses his mind, eventually killing another inmate during a psychotic episode.

Christian Slater plays attorney and recent Harvard Law grad James Stamphill, who's tasked with representing Young in his subsequent murder trial. Stamphill's main argument puts Alcatraz on trial for its unduly harsh conditions, alleging that Young's prolonged separation from others and mistreatment necessarily led to the murder.

In a telling scene, Stamphill seeks the truth about the case from Young, but Young deflects every question, only wanting to talk about baseball, women, and Stamphill's life. Stamphill changes tactics and begins to meet Young on Young's terms, so they talk about baseball, women, and life. With so much discussion about women, Stamphill thinks that providing a prostitute for Young will help Young confide even more in him, but the awkward experience emotionally overwhelms Young. After having no contact with human beings for three years, sex with a stranger is too intimate an experience. From a viewer's perspective, it seems that Young would much rather connect with someone through real conversation, dialogue, and shared experiences rather than a meaningless sexual encounter. Stamphill notices Young's reluctance and anxiety and decides to get to know Young as a person. They began to connect as one human to another instead of one person trying to fix another. Eventually, Young shares more information about what has taken place over the past few years of his life.

As for Young's final verdict, watch the movie.

Murder in the First provides a number of helpful illustrations in regards to the stories we tell ourselves. For instance, the suffering Young endures following his solitary confinement shows the dramatic effects of how isolation affects our brain, social skills, and our basic need for connection. Though we may not suffer from similar, prolonged physical confinement from others, we may often feel disconnected from others, even if they're in the same room with us. This disconnect often happens as a result of the stories we write about our surrounding reality.

Furthermore, Stamphill's attempts to connect with Young provide a short blueprint for how to truly engage with another person: not by forcing your pre-written stories upon them, but by choosing to truly listen to the other person and meeting them where they are. In doing so, Stamphill discovers the key to unlocking Young's well-guarded past. By laying down his own mask, he's able to get Young to willingly lay down his mask as well. That's the point where pretense ends and true connection begins.

ONLY THE LONELY?

Stories like those presented in *Murder in the First* often present us with a heightened version of reality. Our suffering seldom rivals what Young endured, so reason would dictate that our reactions to loneliness wouldn't be as serious. However, in my work as a therapist, relational disconnection has been a constant theme in the counseling sessions. **Despite the rampant number of ways technology touts connecting us—they're called social networks after all—hundreds of my clients still feel disconnected and lonely.**

Like Henri Young, people who don't feel safe in relationships (those who are afraid of getting hurt again) often react to stressful situations in various ways. The actions and posturing I describe below often reveal themselves in people who avoid connection, whether subconsciously or on purpose. They exhibit these particular kinds of defensive behavior because they are scared to be seen and known. They find it difficult to be vulnerable with other people because their past vulnerability has led to pain. Because of that inner wound, they use these defensive maneuvers to form a sort of impermeable, invisible membrane around themselves in order to protect themselves from further harm.

See if you identify yourself or someone you care about in these descriptions:

- **They talk in circles.** When asked a direct question, they offer a surface-level answer that fails to properly address the question. When asked the same question again, they're likely to repeat their first answer, or give some variation on that answer, thus completing a conversational 360-degree turn.

- **They talk in generalities.** When asked a specific question, they reply with a vague answer, seeming to say just enough of the truth to make them feel good about themselves. For instance, if a substance abuser is asked if they've used drugs recently, they may reply, "Nah, my friends and I hung out and stuff. I mean, we did some things that probably aren't the best for us, but it's all good. No one got hurt."

- **They're defensive.** Such replies can often be seen before they're heard. Their body language suggests aggression and/or defensiveness. Answers typically arrive quickly, with an increased volume, and with more animated movement than normal.

- **They're argumentative.** Similar to being defensive, a client who is protecting him or herself by being argumentative may deflect questions directly back to the questioner. For example, when asked "How would you like to begin our session today?" a client may say in a sharp tone, "How would you like to begin our session?"

- **They make jokes.** On the other end of the emotional spectrum, some people will attempt to be light-hearted about their serious issues by cracking jokes or replying with sarcasm. For instance, if someone who's experienced sexual abuse is asked about their sexual history, they may laugh and say, "Well, I played doctor with a friend of mine once!" There's a noticeable disconnect in the gravity of the situation and the levity of the other person's response.

- **They withdraw and avoid.** Questions may be met with long bouts of silence or no answer at all. Scheduled meetings may be coincidentally "missed" on a regular basis. The other person finds any number of excuses in order to avoid facing the stressors of their life.

- **They speak in the second person.** Instead of using "I" statements like "I know what I did was wrong," they use "you" statements like "You know when you do something wrong sometimes, and then . . . ." It's a not-so-disguised way for people to talk about themselves without actually talking about themselves in first person.

While such clients may feel as if their reactions are necessary in order to protect themselves, such reactions have the opposite effect: They reinforce the disconnection and loneliness they already feel. The stories they tell themselves in the mini-dramas they create and narrate on a daily basis in my counseling office form an invisible membrane around their true selves, a cloud of competing voices that fogs up every relationship. It's as if every false story they create is another building block they place in front of themselves to create an impenetrable wall. Two sad consequences to such personal architecture then occur: it prevents anyone from getting in *and it prevents the architect from getting out.*

And here's another conundrum of the lonely. They may say things like, "I've let people get close to me before, and they've hurt me. I can't let that happen again." Truly, if we knew their past hurts we would likely have much greater empathy toward them. Yet it's their self-constructed wall of half-truths—a prison of their mind—that prevents anyone from ever truly knowing their pain. **In order for true connection to occur, the wall must come down, and most of the dismantling work has to be done from the inside out.**

However, once a few light rays begin gleaming through that wall, a helping hand can assist in its demolition.

THE DAYS OF OUR LIES

A caring and careful external presence, like a trusted friend, a close family member, or a professional therapist, can help someone who suffers from loneliness by reaching out to that person and then modeling what it means to seek honest relational connections. Such a relationship comes through not only sharing about the circumstances and facts of our days, but also discussing our experiences of those facts. In psychology and therapy, relational communication has been broken down into two primary levels: content and process.

Content-related conversations share the facts of our days. For example, "I went to the grocery story, then picked up the kids from school, " or "I took a long lunch with a new client today, so I had to stay late and finish up a few things." For many of us, this is often where our conversations both begin and end. **Such content-related conversations are like swimming in the shallow end of the pool.** It's safe and there's little chance we'll ever feel like we're getting in over our heads.

Process-related conversations dive beneath the surface of our days. We share our internal experience of the facts we just relayed. For instance, "When I went to the grocery store today, I heard a song playing that reminded me of our first date. It made me thankful that, even though we've been through a lot lately, we're still together. And when I picked the kids up from school, our son told me he made a B on his math test. With as hard as he's studied lately, I was really proud of him, and I told him so."

Such process-related conversations should also happen when the emotions tied to the experience are perceived as "bad." For example, "That new potential client I had lunch with today could mean huge numbers for me and more money for us. But I noticed my chest tightening and I was feeling anxious because

I wanted to win this new client so badly. I'm a little afraid what might happen if we don't land this client."

You may have felt your own chest tightening just a little while reading that last section. How often do you talk about the emotions, fears, and hopes that sit just beneath the facts of your days? How often do you let those close to you know if you're struggling with raising your kids, or if you and your spouse may be gradually devolving into just becoming roommates and nothing more? How often do you celebrate the milestones within your family and truly tell others how their life brings joy to yours?

Pause here for a moment and rate your typical conversations. What percentage of your conversations are content-related vs. process-related? Are eighty percent just telling others facts and twenty percent telling them about the experience of those facts? Or are you fifty-fifty? Or, do you relish telling others about your experiences? Knowing what you provide to others in conversation is a helpful insight into whether or not you may be building a wall around yourself. Furthermore, understanding the types of conversations you have can help you discover the stories you may be telling yourself about other people in your life. If your conversations tend to stay shallow, you may have already judged another person without knowing their full story. In other words, you've already written a story about them in your mind so you believe that you don't need to have a process-related discussion with that person.

If you discover that your conversations tend to be more content-related, don't lose heart; many people have a challenging time in sharing the experiences of their days. This happens for a variety of reasons, like issues stemming from one's family of origin, socialization, distrust, anxiety, and/or a lack of self-confidence. Remaining on the surface level of conversations is a problem that a majority of people struggle to even notice, let alone overcome.

In other words, even if you feel alone, you're not alone. **To some degree or another, we all fail to effectively communicate the whole truth about our experiences in life.**

When we only provide someone else with the facts of our days, it's not that we're blatantly lying to them, but we definitely aren't providing them with the best picture of that moment. When we remain content with our content-related conversations, we're not adding the emotional details to our stories that are so necessary for true connections. In fact, when we fail to share our deeper experiences of a life event, we're actually providing ripe material for the other person to use in creating stories about us! If you just share the facts of an event, the other person will inevitably try to answer certain questions in their mind about your experience of the event. "Does that mean he's angry with me?" Or, "Does that mean she's depressed?" Without further details, they will fill in the blanks of your story with whatever script they have written for you.

> **When we fail to share our deeper experiences of a life event, we're actually providing ripe material for the other person to use in creating stories about us!**

Are you starting to see how both the stories we tell ourselves and the stories others tell themselves can lead to relational disconnection?

STRANDED ON FANTASY ISLAND

I believe that our most profound aspiration in life is to know and be known by another human being.

With sensitivity to varying spiritual worldviews, the biblical narrative about the Garden of Eden contains some interesting principles about the nature of humankind. It states that we are designed to connect with one another, and God couldn't have been more blunt about it. "The Lord God said, 'It is not good for the man to be alone'" (Genesis 2:18, NASB). Consequently, God gifts Adam with Eve, but relational ruin follows quickly after. The serpent deceives Adam and Eve with a false story. That story leads them to break their fellowship with God and to withdraw from each other by covering their nakedness. **Like Adam and Eve, our twisted narratives have opened cracks between us, and over time those cracks can become chasms that prevent us from knowing, engaging with, serving, loving, and enjoying each other, or, if you will, covering our emotional nakedness.**

Our need to know and be known explains some of our most powerful drives. In our desire to stave off loneliness, these drives can become disordered. For example, pornography tells unrealistic stories that cannot be fulfilled in real life. But, as a therapist who has worked with thousands of clients who choose unhealthy avenues to cure loneliness, I see additional factors at work. Many men and women are driven to a wide spectrum of venues for meeting their emotional needs, like casual flirting, chat rooms, social networks as a hookup haven, pornography, or prostitutes. Of course, these are broken ways to go about truly meeting our innate need for connection. Self-indulgent intents are not always (or even mostly) about sex or romance in the first place. Such substitutes for connection seek to meet a surface-level need without addressing the deeper issues. That's why such behaviors are so addicting yet ultimately unfulfilling.

We deeply yearn for someone to know and accept us, and we long to feel close to another human being. The problem is that the cost for that sort of connection is often too high. Intimacy requires showing up in a relationship with humility and vulnerability as well as with more selflessness and less selfishness. This does not mean that we lose ourselves in this process. There is a balance here of being giving, loving, and selfless, but still standing up for yourself, an issue we'll discuss in Chapter 15.

> **We deeply yearn for someone to know and accept us, and we long to feel close to another human being. The problem is that the cost for that sort of connection is often too high.**

When the immature, self-focused version of us shows up, we want the benefit of an intimate connection without paying the price of setting aside selfish desires. Flirting, connecting with an old flame on social networks and/or pornography dangle the possibility of intimacy without commitment and connection without emotional cost. In interviews, prostitutes say that a surprising number of their customers are men and women who just want to be accepted. Their clientele talk about themselves, their jobs, and what matters to them. They want someone to listen to them, acknowledge their sexual needs, and not reject or laugh at them. Many of these men and women cannot find that acceptance in legitimate relationships because of a difficulty in being known. They feel that they are far too open to being hurt if they actually open up to others (whom they don't have to pay for the opportunity to do so). Additionally, they may also desire to have power and control in a relationship, and the fact that they are the paying customer automatically grants them control that they don't possess in any other sphere of their life.

I'm not condoning these behaviors. I am suggesting that what drives them is grounded in the scripts they've accrued through historical trauma, unmet needs from a primary caretaker (i.e., parents), abuse as a child, or other family of origin issues. Regardless of the many motivations that may tempt a person to seek connection in unhealthy places—these vain attempts at a "true" relationship strand them on an island of their own creation, reinforcing their loneliness rather than actually meeting their deep need for real connection. The story they tell themselves says that an impersonal image on a screen or a hired lover will fulfill the desires of their heart, despite the fact that they know better from past experiences. But, without outside help, these people can get stuck in a cycle that seems to have no exit point.

We all want to know and be known by another human being. It is one of our greatest needs. Our bodies die within days or weeks if we don't have food, water, or sleep—but our souls die without human connection. That's why solitary confinement—whether self-imposed or not—ultimately results in relational ruin.

> **Our bodies die within days or weeks if we don't have food, water, or sleep—but our souls die without human connection.**

ALL BY MYSELF

Any false narratives that prevent people from being genuinely present with each other have the potential to produce loneliness, heartache, and missed opportunities for love and friendship. In other words, **it's not just unhealthy attempts at connection that wreak havoc on relationships; it's *any* story we tell ourselves that fails to properly take into account the other person's real perspective.** Admittedly, some false narratives cause much more damage to relationships than others, but the stories we make up are often what lead to us feeling as if we're alone.

Since we often write these inner dramas while the other person is talking, we don't hear what they're actually saying. We're too busy interpreting their words and actions based on the script we're writing for them in that moment. Such one-sided conversations isolate us. When we write such stories, we can never really get to know the other person, nor they us. We may be standing just a few feet from another person and carrying on a conversation with him or her, but the characters in our minds are the only real company we're keeping.

We're Henri Young in solitary confinement, trapped in our own minds with seemingly no way to escape. Fortunately, there is a way out. Although, you have to go backward before you can go forward.

61

SECTION TWO: THE PROBLEM

"Where do these stories come from?"

SEEKING SAFETY

"You have power over your mind —not outside events.
Realize this, and you will find strength." | Marcus Aurelius

SURVIVAL OF THE SAFEST?

From a very early age, we seek safety, and this innate need to feel safe plays itself out over and over during our lives.

The womb is our first protective barrier to the world at large, an oasis of safety where our every need is met. Then, we're suddenly thrown into the world, attacked by stark lighting and held by strange hands until we lock eyes with the person we believe will continue to keep us safe from all harm: mom. When just starting out in life, a mother's arms become a place of safety. As we grow just a bit older, a pacifier or blankie might become an item that calms us. We gravitate and fixate on these things, especially when troubling circumstances arise. Since we know that these people or items cause us to feel safe, they have a powerful and sometimes subtle way of calming us and helping us to cope with problems that inevitably occur in life.

Eric Erickson's eight psychosocial stages of development begin at infancy. He surmised that the first major crisis a child suffers is trust vs. mistrust, i.e., whether the world is a safe place or a capricious, unpredictable place. Because of a baby's uncertainty about the world at large, they look to their primary caregiver for stability in life. If their caregiver can provide the care the child needs, the child will develop hope and a healthy trust that other people in their life will also help keep them safe. If their caregiver fails to provide a sense of security, the child will develop fear and a lack of trust in others—an emotional burden that will likely haunt every one of their future relationships.

In a similar vein, James Fowler's Stages of Faith lists "Intuitive-Projective" faith as the first stage, meaning that a child, typically between three and seven years old, lives in a highly imaginative, fantasy-laden state. Logic has little to do with their thoughts, and they're free to roam the countryside of their mind for whatever story seems most compelling to them. But because they're within such an inquisitive, curious time of their life, they're highly susceptible to outside influences and examples. If a primary caregiver provides a model for trusting others, a child is likely to adopt that worldview as their own. However, if a mother or father fails to model what it means to trust others, a child's future relationships may suffer as a result.

Eventually, we grow out of those stages, yet our subconscious need for safety never leaves us; it just changes forms. For teenagers, safety might mean fitting in at school. After all, if you can fit in well enough, you can escape bullying and the particular devastations that bullies can impart on a person. Safety in adolescence might also mean seeking a stable home life. Teens who are constantly berated or even abused by their parents won't feel safe at home. Consequently, they seek out other ways to feel safe, whether that's through normative, legal means like hanging out with their friends more often, or through more damaging ways like drug or alcohol abuse. Because they don't feel safe at home, they will seek a feeling of safety in some other way.

For children and teens fortunate enough to grow past those stages, they will still wrestle with safety as adults. Often, adults seek such safety through a committed relationship or stable finances. When a significant other meets their physical, emotional, and mental needs, they will feel safe in the relationship and will seek to nurture that relationship as much as they can. When people no longer feel as if their needs are being met, many will entertain thoughts of going outside of their relationship in order to see those needs met. Adults also find safety in their finances. Though an illusion of safety, a hefty bank account promises financial security. In other words, they're certain that they won't have to worry too much about one of the major concerns of adulthood. Money in the bank makes a people feel safe and protected from whatever life may throw at them.

> **Many adults seek safety through a committed relationship and/or stable finances.**

Now that we've taken a look at some of the ways we've all sought safety throughout our lives, consider what people, items, or issues you run to in order to feel safe. You may be working overtime too often in order to pad your bank account, but all of that extra time may be stealing important moments away that you should be spending with your children. While you may justify your career and financial ambitions by saying that you're working with your children's future in mind, you're currently missing their present and causing them to feel unsafe. These are just a few ways that we desire safety.

Take a few minutes now to contemplate your own ways of seeking safety. Write in the margins or take some notes on your device.

Why do we seek such safety? It's a basic human need, like our thirst for water or our hunger for food, but our inner drive toward safety is not as readily apparent as our need for the other basics of life. It's easy to see that we innately seek safety when physical pain occurs. When a child who doesn't understand how a stove works touches its hot surface, the child's arm immediately pulls back, the nerve endings on their fingers sending immediate and painful responses to their brain signaling, "NEVER DO THAT AGAIN." It should only take one instance of such a painful event for the child to remember how badly that stove hurt them. Though our desire for physical safety is often easily learned beginning with childhood, assessing our need for emotional safety is often more difficult. Yet the reasons we seek such safety parallel why we seek safety from physical harm.

> **Why do we seek such safety? It's a basic human need, like our thirst for water or our hunger for food, but our inner drive toward safety is not as readily apparent as our need for the other basics of life.**

If we've been hurt once, our heart warns us, "NEVER DO THAT AGAIN," but sometimes it's challenging to know exactly what hurt us in the first place. Without properly recognizing and naming the pain that we experienced, we could wander through life behind an impenetrable wall of our own construction, a.k.a, the stories we tell ourselves, to protect ourselves. Since we have a vague notion of how a person once hurt us, we work to ensure that no one else will ever hurt us in the same way again. We seek safety from such relationships, even when we're not quite sure what, precisely, we're seeking safety from.

Here's a quick illustration to that end. After a year of dating, a woman broke off her engagement with her fiancé. Devastated by her leaving the relationship, the man didn't date for the next year, and when he started dating again, he found it impossible to be vulnerable with anyone else. He knew that he kept his conversations surface level, but he didn't know why. He reasoned that it was because he simply didn't feel a connection with whomever he was dating at the time.

If he would have stepped outside of himself for a moment and taken a 30,000 foot view of his romantic life, he would have recognized that the deep pain he suffered in being left by his fiancée caused him to seek safety in his other relationships.

Consequently, he continues to keep all of his new relationships purposefully (though subconsciously) shallow so that *the same thing won't happen to him again.* In other words, the story he tells himself is that any woman he might date won't be interested in a long term relationship. Because of the fear of being hurt again, he refuses to make himself vulnerable in a dating relationship.

You can insert an almost infinite number of variables into such an equation. "Because X happened to me in the past and resulted in Y, I'm never going to let X happen to me again."

- Take a moment and fill in that equation with the deepest pain you've experienced in life.

- Then, consider how you consciously or unconsciously orient your life so that you never have to face such emotional pain again.

- Now, ask yourself what stories you may have made up about others in order to stave off possible, repeat emotional pain.

This should lead you to think about what we first talked about: where do you run for safety? Knowing what you run to—and what you're running from—is the first step in seeking relational healing.

> **Knowing what you run to—and what you're running from—is the first step in seeking relational healing.**

On a cautionary note, our need for connection must still be balanced with our need for individuality. Connection fulfills us, but not if we lose ourselves in the process. If we constantly attempt to try to be who we think other people want us to be, we will not feel whole or emotionally healthy. We will be telling stories to ourselves about ourselves that aren't true. As we progress through this book, you'll learn ways to set proper boundaries in your life so that you can retain your core identity while still seeking to be open, honest, and vulnerable in your relationships.

INTO THE DEEP

Here's the main complicating factor when it comes to seeing people and experiences as equations to be solved: life and people are unpredictable. Attempting to assess someone's motives is like scuba diving. At forty feet below the surface, you may see stunning sea life and fantastic coral, but if you stay longer and go outside your comfort zone, you discover that at seventy feet below the surface the reef stops and a drop off of 5,000 feet lies below you. Had you not done the challenging work to get to that place, you would never have known about that vast, hidden, fascinating environment. Like our relationships, unless you dive deep beneath the surface level, it's impossible to know the full story.

> **Life and people are unpredictable.**

When you meet a person for the very first time, you likely make a snap judgment about that person based on a variety of reasons, like their gender, ethnicity, clothing, body language, speech, smell, etc. We are all guilty of this, and these quick assessments

71

of others are steeped in a number of factors that have affected us over time, like what our family has taught us about certain people groups, or how television portrays particular types of people, or our past experiences with someone who looks similar to the person we've just met.

If only our brains were like a DVR, then we could pause these split-second moments, turn on the closed captioning of our minds, and read through the long list of reasons why we've subconsciously and narrowly defined a new acquaintance as a particular kind of person despite the fact that we know nothing about him or her. In other words, we skim the top of the ocean, but our minds have predetermined what lies beneath the waters.

Why do we do this? Because it makes us feel safe. The stories we tell ourselves about other people can be like wrapping a warm blanket around our scarred, scared heart. These stories—many of which are projections of our own stories onto other people— work to protect us. They also work to grant us interior control of an exterior world that is wildly out of our control, whether we want to admit it or not.

> **The stories we tell ourselves about other people can be like wrapping a warm blanket around our scarred, scared heart.**

THE UNMOURNING MOTHER: A CASE STUDY

One of my favorite quotes on this issue comes from counselor and author Rick Carson: **"Beliefs are opinions that we develop loyalty to over time."** Read that quote again, slowly. Identify a particular opinion you have about someone else, then weigh it against that quote. What opinion about another person has become a petrified belief in your mind? If this quote doesn't quite make sense to you, consider the following case study from my practice.

A CFO in his mid-fifties visited my office after his father's death. Deeply grieved by this loss, he was confused and angered by his mother's apparent lack of grief. Despite having been married to his father for more than fifty years, his mother started dating someone just two months after the funeral. My client had repeatedly attempted to let his mother know his feelings about her actions, but she was always conveniently preoccupied with her new love interest. Because of this, the son reasoned, as many of us would, that his mother wasn't properly grieving such a significant loss. His mind would even wander so far as to think the unthinkable: had she really loved his father at all?

As we worked through the issue, I invited the grieving son to learn how to calm himself through noticing his emotions, quieting his mind, and learning how to redirect his thoughts when he started to write fictional stories. As his anxiety decreased over time, he finally initiated an honest conversation with his mother. A few minutes into their conversation, his mother began to weep, a flood of tears bursting through the dam that she had constructed around her heart. He learned that his mother had been deeply grieving and that her new relationship was just a coping mechanism to help her get over the most devastating loss of her life.

Because my client so ardently believed that his mother wasn't upset about their loss, he developed loyalty to that unfounded opinion, to that story, as the days and months wore on. With each new day, that story became just a bit more solidified in his mind until it became a firm though misguided belief about his mother. Since he told himself this story over and over again, he became its most loyal champion, filling in all of the blanks of his story in order to make sense of what he couldn't control. Until our work together helped to reveal this staunch and unchanging belief about his mother, this particular client couldn't view his mother in any other way. Everything he thought about her was clouded by his over arching belief that his mother had simply moved on with her life. His loyalty to this fabricated story had a profound impact on him and his relationship with his mother.

But, as often happens with the stories we tell ourselves, he was wrong.

LOSING CONTROL

When I talk about problems in life, I typically refer to handles that people are prone to grab. Such handles are the coping mechanisms my clients use in order to make sense of what's confusing or challenging to them. In other words, what's the first thing they reach for when trouble comes their way?

For many, that first handle is control.

There is much in life that is outside of our control, yet the stories we tell ourselves are our vain attempts to control others. Especially when we are being manipulative or functioning in a narcissistic way, we can tell ourselves such a convincing story about another person that *the other person starts to believe the story too.* The other person then obediently acts out their pre-written part for fear of upsetting the manipulative one. This is not a healthy relationship dynamic for either person.

> **There is much in life that is outside of our control, yet the stories we tell ourselves are our vain attempts to control others.**

When we cannot control ourselves, we try to control other people. When our interior world is filled with anxiety, we have three options:

- Manage our anxiety through healthy, life-giving coping skills, i.e., listening to music, spirituality, healthy self-talk, creativity, or exercise.

- Manage our anxiety through unhealthy coping skills, i.e., numbing, escaping or addiction.

- Or we choose to try to control others with the goal of calming our internal anxiety. Our thinking becomes, "If I can control their behavior, then I can feel less anxious."

When we choose number three, we become the director of our own interior movie, and we will order everyone else around as we see fit. We seek to control the uncontrollable through the only medium in which we feel we have complete control: our minds.

Again, this is a safety measure. By controlling others, whether through the narratives in our minds or through actual manipulative behavior in real life, we are ultimately seeking safety. If I can control your life, or at least hold great sway over it, then I can be more confident of obtaining an outcome that's desirable to me. In other words, the stories I write within my mind will always result in my happiness or comfort and never in me experiencing suffering. If I can see to it that these made-up fabrications about others somehow become true in real life, then I can protect myself from being hurt.

> **When we cannot control ourselves, we try to control other people.**

But, despite our best efforts, people are not easily controlled. So how can we learn to live in a vulnerable yet healthy state?

GAINING CONTROL

Because people are unpredictable variables, they must be carefully and constantly observed and understood. How do we know what the people around us are thinking, feeling, and doing? How do we know what they want, or what they might do next? We have to look and listen to them in order to read the clues in their words and demeanor. We need to grasp the larger situation, because what someone feels, thinks, wants, or might do next is often dependent on what the *other* people around them think, feel, want, or do.

All of us at one time or another pay more attention to the stories in our heads than to what's going on around us in real life. The stories in our minds are more interesting, compelling, and controllable than real life. We become so absorbed by what we think is going on that we ignore the real life clues that our story is a fiction or daydream. We miss the real story for the far more engrossing film that's playing within the theater of our minds.

> **The stories in our minds are more interesting, compelling, and controllable than real life.**

As I've said, another way to picture these stories is as scripts for how we think a given situation should play out. We cast ourselves and those around us into roles within those scripts and then try to direct the action. We recite our lines, and when the people we've cast as characters in the scene don't read the lines we've written for them, we get confused and frustrated. We keep trying to force the situation back into our predetermined script, subconsciously goading, coaxing, and coercing others to go where we tell them and say what we've written for them.

Similarly, we can imagine these stories as films that we load and project from our brain onto the inside of our eyeballs. We can't really see or hear what people are actually doing or saying because our vision is blurred by the movie we project onto the situation. Later, we are sure we heard or saw something that in fact didn't actually happen. Again, there's a noticeable and harmful disconnect between what our minds tell us and what actually happened.

Where do all of these stories, scripts, and films come from? In the next few chapters, we'll explore three specific sources of these fictions that keep us from connecting with actual people and what's actually going on around us. We'll see that many of these stories come from our families, the media, or our past experiences.

In later chapters, we'll look at ways to stop giving full weight to the stories we tell ourselves. For instance, being present means really looking, listening, and engaging with what's really going on around us. It means learning when to focus on the inner life, when to tune out external distractions, and when to invert that concentration by tuning out the inner stories, putting aside the inner scripts, and turning off the inner films to get in sync with the external world. I will teach you specific strategies to grow in your ability to live in the here and now.

But, learning these strategies isn't always easy. First, we must do the work of identifying where our stories have come from, and we'll begin with the most challenging origin of them all: *our families*.

FAMILY TALES

"Every marriage is a battle between two families struggling to reproduce themselves." | Carl Whitaker

THE STORIES OUR FAMILIES TELL US

Have you ever experienced a moment where you think, speak, or do something, then immediately put your hand to your mouth and say to yourself, "That's just what my mom (or dad) would do!" Depending on your relational history with your parents, this momentary event may be a shocking revelation or a pleasing reminder. It could be a bittersweet realization of how much you never wanted to be like them, but how much you actually emulate them in your adult life. On the other hand, you may be grateful for the way your parents raised you, thankful that you were afforded a nurturing atmosphere in which to grow.

Whether we're aware of it or not—and even if we may try to actively fight against it—many of the stories we tell ourselves began with the stories our parents told themselves within our earshot. From a very young age, we heard what they said and saw what they did. We also experienced whether or not what they said and what they did aligned. Like a sponge, our young minds soaked up every word, emotion, and action that our primary caregivers said, felt, or performed. Even if we spent our childhood glued to a television set and barely heard what our parents said, our surrounding environment left an indelible mark on our internal scripts.

> **Like a sponge, our young minds soaked up every word, emotion, and action that our primary caregivers said, felt, or performed.**

Often, we can't remember when we first heard these stories because they exist in our earliest, haziest memories. These are the stories your family told you, or modeled for you, when you were a toddler. The grownups talked and some of what they said became the basic narratives that formed an interpretive grid through which we would see the world.

Some stories were blatant: "Don't talk to strangers!" Others were much more subtle, beliefs picked up more through osmosis than anything else, like not trusting other people who seem different from us. As a child with a young and malleable mind, hundreds of such direct and indirect stories would fill your mind, a vast majority of which, you wouldn't have been able to identify as formative beliefs about the way the world works. Even today, you may have some difficulty in seeing back far enough to understand where your earliest scripts come from, but this is an important step to take in order to better understand your own biases when it comes to relational wholeness.

Why is it so challenging to notice our family of origin scripts? Because the most powerful stories we tell ourselves are the ones we don't realize are stories. In other words, some stories are so ingrained in our minds that we take their narrative assumptions as basic premises in our worldview. The beliefs we're raised with often petrify into what we consider immutable facts in our lives. But, these beliefs aren't facts. Consider Rick Carson's insightful quote again: "Beliefs are opinions that we develop loyalty to over time." Since we've lived with the stories of our primary caregivers for so long, we've developed an intense loyalty to them that's almost unshakable. We never think to question these stories because we're completely unconscious of them. We accept what they teach us as facts. When we find ourselves dealing with people and situations, we pull out these long-dormant scripts and act on them reflexively.

> **Because the most powerful stories we tell ourselves are the ones we don't realize are stories.**

Because these are the first scripts we file away in our mental filing cabinets, they are also often the first ones we reach for, even if we're not wholly cognizant of that fact. The stories that surround us in our families of origin become templates we use for the rest of our lives. They help us perceive how the world works and how people might think and behave in a given situation. As we become older children, then teenagers, then adults, we access these early scripts to help fill in the blanks when a situation doesn't make sense to us, or when we want to exert control over a situation so that it might turn out favorably for us.

> **The stories that surround us in our families of origin become templates we use for the rest of our lives.**

As you've already read, we use a wide variety of such scripts to accomplish these purposes, but the pre-written narratives from our family of origin seem to have the most power over us precisely because we're often unaware that we're working off such a primal, long-trusted script. Since these stories seem so intrinsic to our identity, it can often be challenging to separate our family of origin stories from who we really are. If we staunchly believe that the world and its inhabitants behave in particular ways because "we were raised that way," it will be difficult to be a more objective observer when a troubling situation presents itself. And, since both sides in any relationship have their own family of origin stories influencing their behavior, relational impasses can happen quickly but last for a lifetime—and neither party may understand why the other is behaving as they are.

However, if we can learn what family of origin stories influence *our* lives, we can begin to see how our internal scripts affect our relationships.

WHAT IS A PRIMARY CAREGIVER?

Before continuing, it's important to this chapter on families that you understand what I mean by the phrase "primary caregiver." I've used it a few times already, but to be clear, a primary caregiver is not just a mother or a father. While moms and dads are most often a person's primary caregiver, this therapeutic phrase encompasses any person who is responsible for providing care to someone who cannot care for themselves.

In other words, your primary caregiver may have been a grandparent, an aunt or uncle, or even an older sibling. Throughout the rest of this chapter and this book, I will use the terms "mother," "father," and "primary caregiver" interchangeably. If you grew up without a mother or father, simply insert the name of the person or people who were responsible for your primary care as a child and teenager. Regardless of whether your parents raised you or someone else did, the people surrounding you as a child modeled to you how they believed the world works.

As a result, you subconsciously allowed them to write your earliest scripts.

GATHER ROUND: IT'S STORYTIME

The power of family narratives is that they set our default expectations of the way the world around us functions. They are the baseline for how things are supposed to work in our lives. If your family always said a prayer before eating, or kept the television on as background noise at all times, you'll consider those things to be normal and natural. But, when you form internal narratives to explain why your family did those things, those practices go beyond being familiar anchors and become the default stories you use to organize your own experiences.

For instance, did your parents ever argue in front of you? If not, you may believe that healthy families are those who put on a happy face despite any challenging circumstances. We can create a long list of similar questions, from minor to major issues that could still be playing a role in the stories you tell yourself.

Take a few minutes and write down your answers to these questions:

- Did they treat others well?

- Did they prioritize education or religion or work?

- Did your parents express their emotions?

- Did they struggle with addiction?

- Did they show you affection?

- Did they support you emotionally?

- Did they place you in a role as their friend or parent, i.e., a reversal of the order of nature?

- Did they exhibit behavior that was abusive (emotionally, physically, sexually) to you or to your family members?

The answers to such questions form the starting plot to your family of origin narratives. Such stories are most potent when they shape baseline behaviors, like the simple things about how we live. These are scripts we seldom notice because they seem so intrinsic to our lives. They are scripts we learn to follow (or not) when we are very young.

Let's get more specific about some of the following basic narratives we learn as children:

Modeling Family

Did you grow up in a two-parent or single-parent household? If you grew up in a single-parent family, your earliest scripts will be vastly different from someone who grew up with two parents. This does not mean that all children will replicate the home they grew up in, but it is to say that family of origin scripts play a highly influential role in everyone's life.

For you to have a different sort of family than the one you grew up in means that you must rewrite the roles of your most basic, unexamined narratives. In fact, it means rewriting not only the larger story arc of your life, but every chapter and anecdote that comprises that book, from whether or not you eat dinner at the table to whose family you're going to see at Christmas. Those are default scripts you've written based off of what you gleaned as a child from your parents. You memorized go-to lines and learned acceptable behavior by watching your primary caregivers enact certain scenes when you were young. As you age, the path of least resistance when it comes to dealing with a troubling situation is to simply follow the scripts you know so well.

The reason we often get stuck reenacting these scripts (even despite our best efforts) is that it takes work on a daily basis to rewrite our oldest, most trusted family of origin narratives.

Modeling Ambition and Work

As any parent knows, children can be invisible sponges, soaking up whatever's around them and surprising their parents with insightful thoughts or shocking curse words. Because of this natural inclination toward curiosity, children learn about ambition and work ethic from their parents, even if their parents never have a specific conversation with their child about what it really means to have a job.

For instance, did one or both of your parents work? Did you have a parent who worked too much? Or, conversely, did you grow up with a parent who seldom worked at all? When you consider how your parents modeled what it means to have a work ethic, how would you describe what you gleaned from them? Do you work hard now because that's what your parents did, or do you work hard now because that's what they *didn't* do? In either case, your present actions have been subtly influenced by your primary caregivers' modeling of what it means to work. Again, these are ancient scripts stored in your mind that provide an easy way for you to understand how the world works.

The most natural thing for you to do, then, is to reproduce those scenes in your own life. This is one reason why financial wealth or poverty sometimes follows generational patterns. It takes imagination, determination, and effort for someone whose parents had little ambition or work ethic to rewrite both the over-arching script of their life as well as all of the scenes that could lead to a better work life. It is especially difficult when someone's spouse grew up with profoundly different stories about ambition and work. Consequently, each spouse may become exasperated with the other because they can't figure out what's wrong with them. They will render quick judgment—he works too much, she doesn't work enough—without truly understanding the origin of their respective work ethics. Each spouse has a pre-written "work" script for the other, and when one spouse doesn't meet the other's expectations for his or her personal script, conflict happens.

Modeling Money

The stories we tell ourselves based on our parents' ways of living reach deeply into our lives, even into our very pockets. Consider how your primary caregivers spoke about money. When payday rolled around, did they immediately spend it on something nice for themselves or for you? Or did they save money? Did your mom have to ask your dad for permission to spend money, or vice versa? Did you hear argument after argument about your parents not having enough money? Did you always have new clothes or hand-me-downs? Were you ashamed of your house or what you had to wear? Did one parent try to give you money without the other parent knowing about it?

In every instance noted above, your parents modeled what they believed about money. While it may not have made a large impression on your life as a child, as an adult you now understand the financial pressures that your parents had to endure. But, you may be approaching money in the same way that your parents did simply because that's a mental movie you've had for as long as you can remember. Our origins are not necessarily our destiny, but when we find ourselves in similar situations, the most natural thing to do is to pull out the old scripts, read our lines, and expect others to do the same.

Modeling Love and Conflict

Each of the issues mentioned so far are foundational plot points in the stories we tell ourselves based off of the scripts we learned as children. However, the last issue we'll discuss may be the most influential throughout our lives.

When you find yourself in love, what films play in the back of your mind? In other words, how did your parents display their love for each other and for you? Did they model affection? Did they speak well of each other? Did they unduly criticize you or each other? Did they fight with loud and vocal arguments or with silence and slammed doors? Did they throw curses or punches at you or their spouse? Or did they use sarcasm and passive-aggressive behavior to get what they wanted? Did they trust each other? Or were they vocal about their distrust? This list could go on and on, but the main issue I want you to consider is how your primary caregivers modeled love and conflict. Then, think on how their scripts still influence your close relationships today.

I'll keep saying it: your origin is not your destiny. But, especially in love or conflict, when emotions run high, reason is weaker than the old scripts that lie close at hand. Consequently, we tend to replay the scenes because the safety we seek appears to live within those pre-written lines.

Now that we know a few of the broad ways our family of origin stories affect our own scripts, let's look at why these particular kinds of stories seem to be the main root of so much relational conflict.

WHAT WAS IT LIKE TO LIVE WITH THEM?

When I'm digging into the stories my clients tell themselves, and I perceive that their scripts may be stemming from family of origin issues, I ask a very specific but open-ended question: "What was it like to live with your mother?" Or, depending on which primary caregiver has had the most influence on a client (noting that absent caregivers can have an inordinate amount of influence too), "What was it like to live with your father (or grandmother, or sister, etc.)?"

> **What was it like to live with your mother? What was it like to live with your father?**

When my clients respond, they're essentially telling me the stories that they overheard from their parents. They're relating to me the way that their parents modeled life to them. They're allowing me a glimpse into the way their personal stories originated. At the same time, the question works to humanize the primary caregiver, allowing the client to see their parent as a human and not just "my biggest problem" or "my perfect role model."

For instance, let's imagine that Steve and Lauren are my clients. During one of the sessions, Steve voices that he has a tough time connecting on an emotional level with his wife. As a part of the work, let's say I invite Steve into a conversation about his upbringing. He hems and haws about it, voicing his belief that he doesn't see how the two are connected. But, when he rebuffs me, he uses a tone that's more forceful than usual. Sensing that we've discovered a pressure point for Steve, I gently press further into his past at a subsequent meeting, not mentioning his intimacy issues. I ask about his upbringing, then I ask the question that makes Steve hesitate for a long minute:

"What was it like to live with your dad?"

With glistening eyes, Steve tells me that he had a great dad "who was always *there* for me, but was never really there for me, if you know what I mean. He taught me how to play ball and would come to all my baseball games as a kid, even into high school. But whenever we'd talk, the conversation stayed on the surface—centering on sports or his job. I don't recall him saying that he was proud of me, except he did pat me on the back when I was ten, right after I told him I'd punched another kid because he'd made fun of my sister. My dad had a difficult time having conversations about emotions or expressing much emotion. I mean, he was raised that way, so I can't blame him I guess. He loved me in his own way, right?"

The fact that Steve asks that as a question is curious, and part of my role as a therapist is to help people like Steve make the connections that can be so hard to see from a first-person perspective.

In this fictional scenario that plays out all too often in real life, I'd help Steve to see how the stories he learned from his father (e.g., men shouldn't show emotion, men are stoic, men shouldn't show weakness) are the same stories he still unwittingly tells himself. They're the scripts he uses when trying to understand his wife. Intrinsically, Steve thought that "just showing up" and holding down a good job to provide for his wife was enough to make her happy and content. After all, he reasoned, it worked for his mom. So, when Lauren blatantly asks him to share his feelings more often, Steve reads from his dad's script and sarcastically says (while grinning), "*I think I'm* going to head out to the garage and work on my car. We can talk later."

But as long as Steve remains loyal to the opinions of his father, that "later talk" will never happen.

On the other side of the relationship, Lauren must deal with her own family of origin stories. She was raised in a logical home, a place where emotions seldom mattered as much as intelligence did. When she begins to see that her feelings may be altering her decisions, she tries to take a step back from the issue and consider it as logically and objectively as possible. Her single mother had been hurt too many times in dating relationships that she cauterized her own emotional wounds with rational thought, i.e., "I'm too old to date," or "My only purpose now is to raise my child." Since that was the kind of world modeled to Lauren by her mother, Lauren's "yes" to Steve's proposal was based more on facts than it was on her feelings about him.

While Lauren's reliance on her intelligence had served her well in many capacities, it hindered her emotional intelligence. It created problems in her marriage since Steve, on a deep level, believed that all women led with their emotions—something that was modeled to him by his emotive mother. So when Steve seeks an emotional connection with his wife, she's unable to provide that need for him because she often approaches situations from a cognitive, rather than an emotional, viewpoint.

In other words, while Lauren reads from the script based off her mother's take on life, Steve's reading the script he wrote based off his father's take on life. Are you starting to see why our closest relationships can often be the most challenging, and why knowing the origins of the stories we tell ourselves can be extremely important?

Pause here for a moment and try to recall a few of the oldest stories you learned, heard, or saw as a child. *Consider writing down your answer to this question:*

"What was it like to live with _____?"

Be honest but fair. Then, attempt to make some connections between those earliest stories and the ways in which you relate to others in your life. Do you keep going back to these stories in some way? How might rewriting these stories help your relationships?

You may not have an answer for that yet, but by the end of this book, you will be able to identify the stories you tell yourself, the ways those stories hurt your relationships, and how to strengthen your relationships by pressing pause on those incessant, internal narratives.

A CLOSING CAVEAT

For the most part, this chapter appears to condemn much of what your primary caregivers modeled for you as a child. While it's helpful to identify the places where we feel as if our parents may have led us astray in regards to the way the world works, it's just as helpful to notice where our primary caregivers succeeded in modeling relational health. Unfortunately, it's more often the negative aspects of a childhood that result in long-lasting, problematic issues. When we live our lives based off of their faulty scripts, we become stuck in a generational cycle that may eventually influence our own children. That's one of the many reasons we need to learn how to rewrite our own internal scripts.

Note too that I said "rewrite" and not "erase." Try as you might, it's impossible to erase your family of origin scripts. It's like deleting a file from your computer. All it does is go dormant, lying unseen in the trash bin. You can't delete your childhood. It's part of who you are. You can grow, learn, and break negative family cycles, but in order to do so, you have to confront your past, not ignore it.

Keep in mind, the goal of this work is to be observers of our families, notice our points of pain as well as the scripts we write. The goal is not to place blame on our parents, but to take responsibility for how we are going to live our lives.

To be able to rewrite your negative scripts on the fly, you can learn the art of presence, something we'll discuss later on. You can learn how to concentrate on where you are, whom you are with, and what they are actually saying. You can learn to discern what your mom or dad's voice may be saying in your head versus what the person in front of you is actually saying. You can learn to assess whether or not you're working off of a family of origin script. You can learn how to accept your past and extract whatever is valuable from it, as well as how to engage with the present.

When we allow yesterday to be only a guide, we can learn how to walk the less stressful path of the here and now.

STORIES IN THE DARK

"It's funny how the colors of the real world only seem really real when you watch them on a screen." | Anthony Burgess

A BRIEF HISTORY OF TIME AND STORYTELLING

Humans are storytellers, and we have been this way since the dawn of time. Story may be the most captivating and compelling way for knowledge to be passed down to generations, as well as the most entertaining way to pass the time. We cannot help but to make ourselves known through our stories. To be known is a primal urge, and one of our first ways to meet that need is to share our stories with those around us.

> **We cannot help but to make ourselves known through our stories.**

The earliest stories we know of exist in cave paintings, rudimentary drawings made by early humans that tell a basic story of survival. From there, we graduated to the oral tradition, the way that Homer's *Odyssey* was passed down and many of the biblical stories were first relayed. Fast-forward a few thousand years and Johannes Gutenberg revolutionizes the world with the printing press, allowing those early illustrations and the oral tradition to be printed and multiplied as many times over as the ink would last.

A little over one hundred years after that, Shakespeare steps onto the world's stage, putting quill to parchment, penning dozens of plays still performed to this day. Pamphlets, books, and plays proliferate throughout the world, rapidly advancing civilization by disseminating knowledge and entertainment in a way that could never have occurred before.

Drawing closer to the twentieth century, Alexander Graham Bell told a short story of need on the first telephone call when he said, "Mr. Watson, come here. I want to see you."[1] His invention would draw individual men and women, as well as the globe itself, closer together, allowing us all to regale each other with grand stories—or just to while away the day with general chit-chat.

---

1   The First Telephone Call, March 10, 1876, AmericasLibrary.gov

STORIES IN THE DARK

Less than twenty years after that, the Lumière brothers filmed
Sortie de l'usine Lumière de Lyon (Output of the Lumière Factory
in Lyon), credited as the first motion picture. Their basic
invention, along with the hundreds of innovations that would
build upon their work, now allow us to escape the real world by
indulging in cinema. By combining plays with sound and visuals,
movies enhanced storytellers' abilities to captivate audiences in a
way that had never been done before.

In fact, according to film lore, the Lumière brothers' fifty-second
silent film *L'arrivee d'un train en gare de La Ciotat* (The Arrival
of the Mail Train) terrified its audience in 1896. They believed
the image to be so lifelike that they "leaped up from their seats,
screaming, and ran to the back of the screening room."[2] It's
uncertain if that event actually happened, but it's not outside
the realm of possibility considering how new and very different
moving pictures were at the time. This small historical moment
presents a large metaphorical lens for us to use in order to
see the fine line that operates in our minds when it comes to
distinguishing reality versus fantasy.

Thirty years later, Philo Farnsworth showcased the first working
prototype of a television. Eventually, theaters' moving images
would move into our homes, granting us the ability to pass even
more time by succumbing to the powerful nature of stories.
Finding a story you resonated with was as simple as turning a
dial or clicking a button.

Finally, as the twentieth century drew to a close, Tim Berners-Lee
invented the World Wide Web, and it was rapidly adopted the
world over. His revolutionary invention would simultaneously

---

2   Dmitri Vorontzov, "L'Arrivee d'un train, 1895," Vorontzov.com

bring the world closer together and further apart. While email and online messaging services allow us to instantly communicate with each other, sites like YouTube and Facebook have the tendency to steal hours away from us, sometimes siloing us off from real interaction with others.

The Internet, as far as we can tell at this particular moment in the twenty-first century, is the culmination of humanity's need to tell stories. For example, Wordpress.com reports that its bloggers publish *42.6 million* blog posts *every month*.[3] That's 1,420,000 posts *per day*, and that's only one particular slice of users on the Internet. Even taking into account the thousands of likely spam posts, that number is astronomical. It speaks to our innate need to be heard, known, and understood. And why is the Internet such a prime place for our stories? Through its impressive adaptability, the Internet combines every form of storytelling covered in the short history you just read, from images (cave paintings) to podcasts (oral history) to videos (plays, film, and TV) to online communications (phones and social networking).

Best—or worst—of all, you don't even have to get out of bed to consume these stories. Just reach for your phone and nearly every story ever told is instantly available to you.

WHY THE HISTORY LESSON?

Understanding how you write scripts for others based off of stories you already know requires a necessary first step: identifying where those stories originated. In the last few chapters, I have described how our basic scripts often originate from our innate

---

3   Wordpress.com stats

need to feel safe or in control, and from the way our parents modeled for us how the world works. While those issues can sometimes be challenging to properly identify—often because they're so ingrained in a person's psyche due to the scripts' age— this chapter's topic may be even more pernicious because it's so overwhelming and all-encompassing. We may not even realize how much we're influenced by mass media and contemporary culture.

For instance, every storytelling invention didn't eradicate the invention that preceded it. The printing press didn't stop people from verbally telling each other stories. Television didn't shut down movie theaters. So far, the Internet has yet to supplant books, phones, TV, and film (though given enough time it may have the power to do so). **As these mechanisms for story have proliferated, so too have the number of ways in which stories infiltrate our lives, often skirting past our best defenses without our notice.** On a daily basis, we breathe in stories like air. Even more shockingly, the stories we consume through mass media are only one of the many ways we're influenced by much more than the real person across from us in any given situation.

> **On a daily basis, we breathe in stories like air.**

The point I'm driving toward is something you may feel intuitively rather than know logically. And oftentimes our feelings know more than our minds do.

WE ARE VORACIOUS MEDIA CONSUMERS

If you're still not convinced that mass media holds an inordinate sway over your subconscious, let's consider some rudimentary calculations. According to a 2011 report by the American Academy of Child & Adolescent Psychiatry, children watch an average of three to four hours of television every day.[4] Let's take the low end of that average and estimate how much television a five-year-old will consume over the next twenty years of his or her life:

- 3 hours of TV x 365 days = 1,095 hours of TV per year

- 1,095 hours of TV per year x 20 years = 21,900 hours,

- or 912.5 days,

- or nearly 2.5 *years* of TV

Now, let's take that disturbingly high number and multiply it by the number of stories a viewer might digest during a single hour of TV. Again, we'll use a conservative estimate, but we must keep in mind that TV episodes and movies can tell multiple stories, newscasts can showcase dozens of stories in an hour, and each and every commercial tells its own story too. So, on average, let's assume fifteen discrete stories per hour, a majority of which are likely ads.

In that case, by the time an average, three-hour-a-day, TV-watching five-year-old turns twenty-five, he or she will have consumed 328,500 stories, or roughly forty-five stories per day.

---

4   American Academy of Child & Adolescent Psychiatry, "Children And Watching TV, No. 54, December 2011," aacap.org

And that's *only* through TV.

OUR MENTAL MOVIES

If you could slip into a back row seat inside the theater of Steve's mind for a day, you'd likely be shocked by the overwhelming number of film clips he plays on a consistent basis. Minus the context of what's actually going on in Steve's real life, his mental reel of favorite stories and scripts would seem disjointed, and maybe even schizophrenic, to an outside observer. As situations change in Steve's reality, his mind pulls up yet another story that would seem to fit the situation at hand, a pre-written script he can use to help assess the situation. He may flip through his "safety" and "family" scripts first, but if he can't find one that will help him out in his present situation, he may turn to his next best source of information: mass media.

As an example of mass media's wide appeal, film can grasp and hold sway over our imaginations like few other narrative engines. In 2012, more than two-thirds of Americans and Canadians over the age of two saw at least one film in the theater. Additionally, the average moviegoer for those countries bought six tickets that year.[5] Note that this number doesn't take into account home viewing of movies. Studios can rake in hundreds of millions of dollars in a week, and money keeps pouring into that industry as films become DVDs and online streaming rentals. Note too that the pornography industry makes millions more than the traditional film industry, a telling indictment of our inclination toward visual fantasy. The absurd amounts of money that many films make allow more films to be made, and the cycle continues.

---

5   Theatrical Market Statistics 2012, mpaa.org

Why are movies such big business? Because we crave stories. Movies have been described as "larger than life," a phrase that reveals how we sometimes see our lives in comparison to the lives we see portrayed on the silver screen. Consequently, we may say that we're going to an afternoon flick to escape from our reality, but subconsciously we may be attending in order to accrue more scripts for our relational arsenal.

Think that's a stretch?

THE LOGLINES OF OUR LIVES

When screenwriters compose scripts, the entertainment industry demands that their film has a logline. Though a technical term most often used solely in regards to screenwriting, a logline is essentially an elevator pitch for a film. It's a "one or two sentence summary of your film that not only conveys your premise, but also gives the reader emotional insight into the story as a whole."[6]

For instance, see if you can guess the name of the following five films based on their loglines as quoted from the Internet Movie Database (IMDB.com):

- "Two imprisoned men bond over a number of years, finding solace and eventual redemption through acts of common decency."

- "The aging patriarch of an organized crime dynasty transfers control of his clandestine empire to his reluctant son."

---

6 Noam Kroll, "How to Write the Perfect Logline: And Why It's As Important as Your Screenplay," Indiewire.com

- "Set in unoccupied Africa during the early days of World War II, an American expatriate meets a former lover, with unforeseen complications."

- "Two business rivals hate each other at the office but fall in love over the Internet."

- "A Phoenix secretary steals $40,000 from her employer's client, goes on the run and checks into a remote motel run by a young man under the domination of his mother."

In order, these popular films are *The Shawshank Redemption, The Godfather, Casablanca, You've Got Mail, and Psycho*. Due to the loglines' necessary brevity and vagueness, some of those films may have been challenging to guess. But, you probably knew most of them.

For better or worse, we live in a world over-saturated with story, and we often subconsciously allow films' plot lines to become the loglines of our lives. It's not that this is necessarily a bad way to interact with the world around us, as stories also inspire and encourage us to accomplish goals, but when we begin to *only* interact with others based off of the plagiarized, pre-written scripts in our head, our real life relationships will consequently suffer.

If you're struggling to see how "just a movie" might actually affect your real life relationships, let's take a seat in Steve and Lauren's mental movie theaters. Let's go back in time to years before they ever met each other, when each of them were still children and bugging their respective parents to let them watch a film just one more time.

CINEMATIC MEMORIES

"But son, you've already watched that movie twenty times or more. You don't need to watch it again. You quote it all the time for goodness' sake."

"Please Mom? Just one more time? I promise I'll get my chores done when it's over. And my grades will get better. And I'll make dinner."

Steve's mom laughs. "Don't make promises you can't keep, dear. I'll let you watch it one more time, then you have to do your chores. I'll watch with you if that's okay."

"It's okay Mom, but you might not like some parts. There's guns."

"Oh, I'll be okay. I just worry about you, always watching these old Westerns. I'm not sure it's good for an eight-year-old to watch that kind of stuff."

Steve rolls his eyes. "Mom, it's just a movie."

———————

"You want to watch it again? Right now? We just finished watching it!"

"Please, Daddy? It's my favorite Disney movie. Don't you just love how it ends? I could watch it all day long!"

"Don't I know it. Honey, we really don't have time to watch it again."

STORIES IN THE DARK

Slowly, eight-year-old Lauren looks up at her dad with wide eyes she knows he can't resist.

"Okay. Fine. I give up. You win. One more time, but that's it! Then it's your bedtime."

"Thank you, Daddy. You're the best."

"You know real life isn't like these movies, don't you sweetie?"

"Of course, Daddy. Real life is better because it lasts longer!"

Lauren's dad laughs as he starts the movie. He doesn't reply, not wanting to squelch his daughter's naive joy.

When Steve was young, he was infatuated with Westerns. From *The Good, the Bad and the Ugly* to just about any John Wayne flick, Steve couldn't get enough of the classic tropes of those films: shootouts at high noon, damsels in distress, the triumph of good over evil, the strong but silent gunslinger from out of town. With so many repeated viewings, he could quote hundreds of lines from his favorites. And, every word and action in those films became another script stowed away in his mind for future use. He knew he'd never be a real gunslinger when he got older, but he knew what kind of man he wanted to be.

As for Lauren, her first introduction to her all-time favorite film, *Sleeping Beauty*, also happened at an early age. The story of a gifted princess awakened from a perpetual sleep by true love's first kiss captured both her heart and her imagination. Her parents grew weary of her singing, "*You love me at once / The way you did once upon a dream.*" In her young mind, the Disney classic painted the first picture she'd ever truly known of what love looks like between a man and a woman. She wanted to be attractive and talented and someday swept off her feet by a chance encounter with the man of her dreams. Like Sleeping Beauty, she thought she may have to endure a fleeting moment of suffering, but then her prince would come and they would live, of course, happily ever after.

But then Steve and Lauren grew into adults, met and married each other, and put away their childhood fantasies.

Or did they?

GREAT EXPECTATIONS

When Steve and Lauren first started dating, Steve was unknowingly working off the script he'd compiled from many different sources, including his many years of watching Westerns. When other guys seemed interested in Lauren, he'd set himself as her protector, even going so far as to confront these other men. Steve would sometimes hope that Lauren would be in trouble of some kind so that he could save the day and truly prove his love to her. He expected her to be like the leading ladies of the films he loved: attractive but demure, needy but not helpless, and devoted only to his happiness and well-being. Steve would never say these things outright, and he'd likely not even be able to notice how those old films were directing his present actions, but they were scripts that he was accessing in order to assert control over his life.

But Lauren didn't conform to Steve's old-world expectations. As an intelligent woman, she couldn't play dumb if she tried. She was self-sufficient, so she wasn't helpless. And, while she was falling in love with Steve and wanted him to be happy, that was not her sole concern in life. Lauren was a real person, not some two-hour fantasy character held together with a few spoken lines and no backstory. Yet Steve had subconsciously tried to conform her to his image of the ideal woman based in part off of the scripts that he had gleaned from so many Westerns.

Likewise, Lauren had unwitting expectations for Steve based in part off of classic Disney scripts. When Steve said he would never dance with her, she took that as a sign that he didn't really love her, since every prince dances with his princess. When Steve's income required that Lauren had to work as well, her expectations of financial security faltered. After all, a princess doesn't have to worry about money. When Steve showed fear about their future together, Lauren's perception of his confidence wavered. They were going to live happily ever after and that was that.

A COMPLEX ISSUE MADE SIMPLE

These illustrations are purposefully simplistic. Because we swim in story soup, if you will, boiling away excess stories helps us to see how particular stories from films can influence us. **In reality, every story we hear or see becomes another script in our mental filing cabinet, and often these scripts get combined with others we've already stored away.** Essentially, I'm reiterating the point that Steve and Lauren are not solely influenced by Westerns or Disney movies, but they are influenced by a wide array of stories, and those two types of films are small samples of the whole.

There's a subtle lesson within this illustration that also shows how the stories we tell ourselves are like Russian nesting dolls, where one story sits inside of another. Eventually, Steve noticed why he gravitated toward Westerns' portrayal of what it means to be a man. His father lived like one of those men: strong, aloof, silent, unemotional, imposing, distant, and ready to split town if the situation went south. So, when Steve thought about the kind of man he ought to be, the scripts he'd written for himself were filled with lines and actions from his own father as well as the men he'd seen on those Westerns.

As a result, assessing our own stories' origination points can be challenging because similar stories can have multiple beginnings. But doing the work of noting where these stories come from can help you learn how to best rewrite those narratives so that you can relate to the real people in your life and not just the fantastical characters in your mind.

By identifying the ways mass media influences the stories you tell yourself, **you may not go riding off into the sunset living happily ever after, but you will start to live life on a much deeper and more meaningful level.**

THE PAIN OF THE PAST

"Self-reflection is a humbling process. It's essential to find out why you think, say, and do certain things . . . then better yourself." | Sonya Teclai

WHEN THE GROUND FALLS AWAY (PERSONAL EARTHQUAKES)

When she was thirteen years old, Lauren's parents divorced. At the time, she was told few details about it other than learning the phrase "irreconcilable differences." For the next five years, Lauren stayed with her mom and visited her dad every other weekend. Both parents did well in keeping details of their divorce away from Lauren. They also didn't speak ill of their ex in front of her. Though the divorce caused Lauren much anxiety, she learned to cope with it by seeking acceptance with her friends and finding security in good grades with the hope of attending an above-average college.

However, during her last year of college, Lauren came home early for Christmas break. As she unlocked the door to her childhood home, she heard her mom on the phone, talking to her oldest friend. Lauren only heard one side of the conversation, but it was enough for her to figure out every word that was likely being said.

"Can you believe it's been ten years, Jennifer?"

"I know, but you really need to put the past in the past. This is a strange anniversary to celebrate."

"I'm not celebrating. I'm just noting the fact that it's been ten years since I found out about Robert's affair. I can't believe he's still with that woman too!"

As soon as Lauren heard that line, she slowly and quietly walked back through the front door and out to her car. Her quickly rising heartbeat provided fuel for her racing mind. She felt tears begin to form, but she was too shocked to cry. Her anxiety went through the roof. She had just learned what she never knew before, a fact that had been hidden from her for ten years: her father had cheated on her mother. The man she thought she knew so well immediately transformed into a stranger that she wanted little to do with, someone she could no longer trust.

In that singular moment, in the span of just a few minutes, the solid ground beneath Lauren's feet fell away.

Steve loved his first job out of college. As an IT professional with a business degree, he was excited to work for a large corporation that promised good pay, better benefits, and the opportunity to climb the corporate ladder. He saw how, if he could achieve promotions every three years, Lauren would be able to stay at home to take care of their children, something he had always wanted to be able to provide to his wife. Though the hours were long and the stress could reach unhealthy levels, Steve always reminded himself of why he chose this job, as well as the many benefits of staying on long term with such a secure corporation. As a hard and capable worker, Steve was promoted to manager after three years as a staffer. His professional life was aligning with his goals and ambition. His career was going as well as he could have ever hoped.

But then, three years later, the rumors started.

"Did you hear they're thinking of downsizing this quarter? Sales are starting to slip."

"I heard we're going to be bought out. The C-level execs could stand to make some big money if they cash out now."

"Bob in accounting just got let go. It was brutal. Poor guy didn't even see it coming, and he's got two kids about to go into college."

On hearing this, Steve's mind went into overdrive, attempting to vet every rumor through his own conversations with other managers and routinely checking the company's stock price. He'd read every corporate memo twice just to make sure he wasn't missing anything in between the lines. He knew he was edging on professional paranoia, but he was on the edge of another promotion. If he lost his job now, it would be catastrophic.

As more and more people were being quietly let go over the next six long weeks, Steve's mind raced with every negative possibility that could befall him: *I'm going to get fired. I'll lose our health insurance. I won't be able to find another job like this one. We won't be able to afford a child, and we said we'd start thinking about having one soon. Lauren will be ashamed of me.* He wanted these stories to stop, but they dominated his working days so much that it was often the only thing he heard, even when he was talking to someone else. The entire company was wrapped up in "what-ifs."

Then, with all the fanfare of a new email message, Steve read a company memo that made clear what had been obfuscated for so long: the company was being bought by a larger competitor. Steve read the memo three times, then researched the other company, despite the fact that he knew all about them. With this new information, his thoughts became a bit more positive, sometimes wondering what kind of position he might have in the new merged company. Still, echoes of doubt bounced off the walls of his mind: *What if they fire all of the managers because the new regime wants their own people in place? Am I even good enough to keep around?*

One day prior to the outside company's takeover, the Senior VP called Steve into her office. She was smiling, and they had enjoyed a good professional rapport with each other over the last few years. Still, Steve was wary that something wasn't quite right. He didn't hear everything she said in their brief meeting, but he was able to decipher the words "new management," "We have to let you go," and "Just know that it's not personal Steve. It's business."

In that singular moment, in the span of just a few minutes, the solid ground beneath Steve's feet fell away.

INVISIBLE SCARS

It's an unfortunate reality of the world we live in: live long enough and you will suffer. You will experience a grave calamity, an injustice, a wound. You will be hurt by someone you trust. You may wonder what you did to deserve it. You may wail at God or the universe, angered by your suffering or the suffering of someone you love. You will experience loss, whether through death, divorce, or a broken friendship, and that loss will transform how you engage every other person in your life, as well as how you see yourself and how you view the world.

These painful events leave lasting scars. **While some suffering results in physical wounds that all the world can see, every painful episode in your life leaves an emotional wound that's often hidden from view.** Some of us are more adept than others at covering up these internal hurts, while others struggle to free themselves from a deep wound that seems to engulf every fiber of their being. We react to inner pain in different ways, but we all have one thing in common: at some point in our lives, we've been hurt. Since those inner wounds often take much longer to heal than a broken bone does, we learn to walk with a barely noticeable limp. It's not perceptible to others, but we know the particular pain points of our souls, those places we shield off from others because, if they ever draw near to it, they may hurt us in the same way we were hurt before. Because that prior wound was so painful or traumatic, we learn ways to prevent our relationships from ever touching that nerve again.

In fact, we're often so adept at cauterizing the interior wounds through a wide variety of means that we don't notice our long-dormant emotional pain until we have another experience that parallels the earlier trauma. Then, our minds suddenly transport us to the past and how badly we were hurt then. From there, we attempt to tell the future, guessing that the person in our current situation is likely going to hurt us in the same way. As I've said before, we start to build walls around ourselves in order to protect what we feel has already been damaged so badly. We refuse to let other people into our lives because we've been hurt by those in our past who we've let through the proverbial gates of our mind.

To tie this into our grander theme, we suddenly find ourselves relating to the stories in our head about our past suffering and not to the people directly in front of us. We begin to cast our spouse as a former boyfriend or girlfriend who suddenly dumped us for no reason. We begin to fill in every possible blank about a confusing and possibly painful situation with the results of what happened to us the last time we found ourselves in a similar predicament. In other words, we're looking for firm ground when tremors of a possible earthquake start shaking us. Again, it's our basic need for safety and security. When we begin to feel as if we're losing control of a specific sphere of our life, like our career, our finances, our children, or our spouse, we want to grab onto anything that will provide stability. Consequently, we look to the stories we tell ourselves to make sense of an unknown future or an uncertain present. For most of us, the most challenging stories to notice are the ones that have caused us the most pain. We don't want to revisit those experiences. We may have even been told to "keep the past in the past," just like Jennifer told Lauren's mom in this chapter's opening illustration. But that's not a healthy suggestion. When we fail to properly process our past hurts, we're setting ourselves up for future pain, whether such pain is inflicted upon us—or we're the ones inflicting it on others.

> **We look to the stories we tell ourselves to make sense of an unknown future or an uncertain present.**

HOUSE OF PAIN

Because the presence of pain in our lives is such a delicate topic, one that can take considerable time to properly process, it may be helpful to consider how you've been hurt. While the stories and repercussions I've shared in this chapter are not extensive, you may still be able to locate yourself and your invisible scars in those characters. On the other hand, you may be aware of the inner pain you struggle with on a daily basis. In either instance, it's helpful to take a broad approach to naming your past pains so that you might be able to address every issue and not just the one that seems most devastating. As I said before, every event that causes suffering leaves a wound of some kind. If a doctor cannot locate a physical wound, there's no way he or she can work to heal it. The same can be said for our emotional wounds, though they're often much more difficult to detect.

For instance, Lauren was deeply wounded when her parents divorced, then hurt further when she learned the truth as to why they divorced. As rampant as divorce is reported to be in the U.S., it's not surprising that many of my clients wrestle with the relationship they have with their divorced parents. Many articulate how their unstable childhood home affects their own marriage and home life as an adult. When a divorce occurs, for many it can be as if an emotional IED has exploded, shooting shrapnel into every person in close proximity. Extracting such emotional fragments can sometimes take a lifetime. Consequently, Lauren has significant distrust of men in general because her father hurt her and her mother so badly. Until she learns how to battle the stories in her head with the practice of being present, she'll likely never experience true relational intimacy with Steve.

For Steve, his world exploded when the company he worked at for almost nine years "let him go" with barely any notice. Despite that fact that he was well aware of the corporate, faceless nature of his job, he still thought his rapport with his superiors would somehow save him from the company bloodbath. But when the realities of his new, jobless situation settled in, Steve experienced a deep depression. He couldn't bring himself to even look for work, and he definitely didn't want to go into another corporate job for fear of the same event happening again. He was professionally paralyzed, and the pain of the firing struck a near catastrophic blow to his identity. After all, who was he if he wasn't working? Consequently, it would be many years before Steve began to trust his superiors at his new job. His past experiences made it difficult for Steve to work with others and played a role in his anxiety about financial security. The pain of being fired from a job he loved changed who he was on a deep and almost imperceptible level. Until Steve learns how to fight against the painful stories of his past with the actual realities of his present, he'll likely never be free from the anxiety that visits him throughout the day.

While divorce and job loss are two common sources of pain, there are hundreds more. What's more is that these painful moments don't necessarily have to be large-scale hurts or losses. For instance, a business partner of yours may make a unilateral decision without your input, and when the decision proves to be a poor one, both of you must suffer the consequences. Or, one of your children lies to you, a sign that they either don't trust you or don't think that you are smart enough to catch them in their lie. Or, you discover that two of your closest friends have been gossiping about you. What you thought was shared in confidence with one of them has now been aired out for all the world to hear. While each of these examples can hurt people to varying degrees, it's important to note that these experiences are painful no matter the level of hurt they may actually experience. These experiences become further stories that we file away in our now overflowing mental filing cabinets. So, the next time that "friend" comes over to talk, it's likely she will receive polite but rather curt answers.

Because you're working off the script of having been hurt before, you run away from the present opportunity to mend the relationship. Because, let's face it, that's much more challenging to do than allowing your past hurts to dictate a conflict-free relationship. **Like weeds in a garden, these small emotional wounds grow with persistence, and they can eventually take over our interior selves.**

Furthermore, our minds seldom know the real story of particular situations because of our traumas, hurts, or negative relationships from our past. Because we want to somehow make sense of what confuses, frustrates, or has the ability to hurt us, our minds and bodies default to a fight-or-flight response. We will either act very defensively through anger, rage, or high reactivity, or we will withdraw from that person, isolate ourselves, or become a passive party in that relationship. While those are natural reactions to troubling circumstances, they don't lead to less stress or relational health. In fact, our fight-or-flight responses often leave us with more stress and can put a constant strain on our relationships. Those are two reasons why it's important to identify past traumas, especially the ones that may have been with you since childhood.

Traumatic childhood events often leave the largest and longest lasting scars. Like we heard from Steve, his father was physically present but emotionally absent during Steve's formative years. For many Baby Boomers with stoic Silent Generation parents, this type of family life was normative. It's quite telling that those born between 1925 and 1945 have been named "The Silent Generation" as well. During this time, it was commonly understood that children should be seen and not heard. Children with parents who speak little about their emotions save those scripts for future use and may turn into the silent parent they resented having in the first place.

> **Traumatic events that occur to us in childhood often leave the largest and longest lasting scars.**

Even more damaging than the message that children should be seen and not heard are the sufferings of children who endure verbal, physical, or sexual abuse at the hands of someone more powerful than them. Without therapy or a trauma recovery program, those who have experienced child abuse are prone to wrestling with those issues for the rest of their lives.

Sadly, verbal, physical and/or sexual abuse press pause on the development of the emotional and psychological parts of the self, while consistent nurture, stability, and safety enhance development. Those who suffer from abuse at the hands of someone more powerful tend to struggle with feelings of helplessness and powerlessness and, as a result, look for ways to cope with those feelings through numbing, escapism, or addiction. When children receive these kinds of scripts at a young age, their perspective on the way people function becomes greatly altered.

Lastly, it's not just chronic and routine troubling issues that can negatively affect a childhood. Unfortunately, even a child with supportive and caring parents is not immune from pain and suffering. For example, a one-time tragic event during childhood can plague a person well into adulthood. Maybe the child got lost in a busy shopping center, unable to find his mother for several hours. Maybe the child lived through a harrowing car accident. Maybe the child's otherwise healthy father suffered a sudden heart attack and passed away. These kinds of events, though not stemming from a primary caregiver's behavior, can also inflict pain on a child. They are the kinds of circumstances that can happen to anyone at any time, and as adults we sometimes forget—whether through willful denial or true loss of memory—that these singular moments drastically altered the way we thought the world was supposed to work.

So, if the past pain in our lives influences the way we treat others (and ourselves), how can we learn to notice the pain without giving into it? That is, how can we acknowledge how our past pain has developed into a story that we tell ourselves without allowing that story to distort our present reality?

PROCESSING PAIN

We all have pain and even cause pain at different times in our lives. I clearly recall a scenario where I took a step back and processed pain with my children. Running late for one of my boys' soccer games, I made several failed attempts to get my boys to hurry out the door and get in the car. Eventually, I lost it and started to yell—not one of my proudest moments. As we drove to the game and all became much calmer, I apologized to them for yelling. They both responded, "It's okay, Daddy."

In that moment, I decided to take another step beyond simply apologizing for my impatient, aggressive words. I asked them, "What was it like for you when I yelled at you?" In tandem, they said it was "sad" for them. On a small yet important scale, I was helping them to process their pain before it could take root in their hearts and minds. By acknowledging both their pain and my own contribution to their pain, I was working to help heal our relationships before bitterness or disrespect would begin to burrow into them *and me.*

The simple act of acknowledging and verbalizing our pain helps our pain subside. Furthermore, it works to remove emotional blockages that occur with unprocessed pain, like the angry person who refuses to air their grievances and eventually erupts at an innocent bystander. Like mounting pressure, unprocessed pain always finds a release valve. When children who have been physically, sexually, or emotionally abused find no way to effectively process the pain that they've endured, they are much more likely to discover harmful ways, like addiction, acting out, or isolating themselves, in order to negate or numb their inner feelings. On the other hand, when abused children are granted the opportunity to freely talk about the abuse with a safe parent or trusted adult, they are much less likely to reenact that pain in indirect ways as teenagers and adults.

> **The simple act of acknowledging and verbalizing our pain helps our pain subside.**

What specifically do I mean by processing pain? More often than not, processing pain simply means telling a trusted person about the painful event and how you felt about that event. In doing so, the chances of successfully working through the pain increase and the fictional stories you weave around that event will lessen. In talking about your pain with a trusted friend or counselor, you are unburdening yourself of a weight that only gets heavier with time. When we remain silent about troubling matters, we run the grave risk of allowing that past pain to distort and disturb our relationships. When we internalize trauma and try as hard as we can to hide our invisible scars, we do more damage to ourselves—even though we believe that we are simply protecting ourselves from further hurt. Furthermore, if we don't process our pain in healthy ways, we will create our own stories to make sense of the past.

> **When we internalize trauma and try as hard as we can to hide our invisible scars, we do more damage to ourselves—even though we believe that we are simply protecting ourselves from further hurt.**

Another way I like to put it is that we must digest the pain. Especially in cases of chronic abuse, such devastating pain cannot be digested all at once. It must be dealt with bite by bite. For children who have suffered much between the ages of four and six, such digestion occurs over and over again in each developmental stage. In other words, they re-grieve the same pain multiple times as they age. They will experience the cycle of grief—denial, anger, bargaining, depression, acceptance—as young children, then as older children (five to ten years old), then after hitting puberty, and then again in their late teens. If the child is never helped to digest their pain in each developmental stage, it's likely that the pain of their past will greatly influence their adult relationships and emotional health. This is why it's important to help a child who's suffered to process their pain as early as they're able to, as well as to continue to help them process as they become older and re-grieve the same issue. This revisiting of the same issue over the years is more important in a child's life than an adult's because adults don't endure such big developmental shifts as children do.

When we fail to properly process our pain, we will either "act in" or "act out." Acting in oppresses and depresses us. It's a withdrawal from relationships, signified by depression, apathy, and a lack of desire for living life. Acting in amplifies the negative voices in our head, allowing our past pain to define us as someone who deserved to be hurt. On the other hand, acting out attempts to numb ourselves or escape our circumstances. Acting out could mean replacing our pain with self-medicating through drug, alcohol, eating, or sex compulsive behavior. It could lead to a generally combative and defensive position in relationships. Instead of withdrawing from relationships, acting out tries to hide our pain beneath a facade of selfish living. Acting out amplifies the over-confident voices in your head, seeking to replace your past pain with any kind of person or experience that can make the problem go away, even if only for a moment.

> **When we fail to properly process our pain, we will either "act in" or "act out."**

FROM THE PROBLEM TO THE PROMISE

To sum up, one of the major influences on the stories we tell ourselves is past pain. If we don't get clear on the origin of the pain as well as learn how to properly process this pain, our relationships will suffer. We will use these painful scripts to protect us from further harm, shrinking back from circumstances we perceive to be similar to those that once caused us to hurt. If we continue to hide our invisible scars and not allow others to truly know where and how we've suffered, we run the risk of forever alienating the closest relationships in our life. We will also live with anxiety like an unwanted roommate.

Thus far, I've presented you with the premise and the problem of the stories we tell ourselves. The premise is that we do in fact tell ourselves stories all the time. The problem is that these stories can wreak havoc on our relationships and thoroughly increase our daily anxiety. In the following chapters, we will discuss the promise and the practice. If you can learn how to rewrite the stories that you tell yourself, what can you look forward to in your relationships? How will they change for the better? Lastly, we'll discuss the steps and strategies you can take to lessen anxiety, learn the art of being present, and discover how to be a person of presence. Though these suggestions sound simple—and they are—they take a vigilant awareness in order to establish "being present" as a daily relational exercise.

> **If we hide our invisible scars, we run the risk of forever alienating the closest relationships in our life.**

For now, let's look at how your relationships can change for the better and your anxiety over life's troubling issues can lessen.

SECTION THREE: THE PROMISE

"I can really calm my anxiety?"

SHIFT HAPPENS

"Incredible change happens in your life when you decide to take control of what you do have power over instead of craving control over what you don't." | Steve Maraboli

THE SCARE OF A LIFETIME

Two years after their daughter Emma had left for college, Lauren was diagnosed with Stage 3 breast cancer. She had no family history of the disease, so she was fortunate that a screening caught the illness. While the cancer was already advanced, the tumor had yet to spread to any other major organs. Still, her doctors advised her to undergo a double mastectomy in order to prevent the cancer from spreading further. Equally shocked and scared by the abrupt news, she was willing to do whatever her team of medical advisors suggested. A little less than three weeks after her diagnosis, she was in a hospital bed waiting to be wheeled into surgery. Though she only had to wait thirty minutes, the swirling thoughts in her mind made it feel like hours.

If I don't make it out of this surgery—or if this surgery doesn't help and the cancer still takes me—what will become of Steve? Of Emma? Do they know how much I care for them? What are the last words I spoke to them? I've known Steve for more than half my life now, but do I really know him? Was I the best wife for him? Why didn't I try harder? Will he still want me after this surgery? Will he be able to take care of me if this gets worse? Was I a good mom? I think Emma's going to turn out okay, but I wonder if I really gave her the time she needed with me. I hope she's not as distrustful of guys as I was at her age. And I hope she doesn't always rationalize everything like I do. I wish I could have been a more emotive person. I've always had a hard time sharing my emotions. I wish I would have told Steve and Emma more about how I felt—when I was happy, when I was sad. Heck, I should have told them when they upset me too. I just never wanted conflict though, so I'd just rationalize and justify everyone's actions, even my own. Makes me feel like I never really connected with people. Why am I just now seeing this? Please God let me have a second chance. Please let me get through this alive, not so that I can be selfish anymore, but so that I can really get to know the people in my life and let them know how much I really love them. I don't want to have wasted my life. Please God . . . please.

To her surprise, Lauren found herself sobbing, something she hadn't done since she thought Steve was cheating on her. When the medical assistants arrived to take her into surgery, she didn't even try to stop crying. She faced the true and deep pain of her situation and allowed herself to feel remorse for the shallowness of her relationships. Before the anesthesia took its full effect, she thought to herself, *Just another chance God. Just one more.*

During Lauren's surgery, Steve sat in the waiting room, lost in his own confusing, depressing thoughts.

I can't lose her. After all we've come through, all we've fought for together? What was the last thing I said to her? I can't even remember. Was I a good husband to her? Did I ever really listen to her, or was I just always waiting to hear what I wanted to hear? Was she happy? Is she scared right now? I'm scared and I'm not even the one in surgery. What will she look like after the surgery? Stop that Steve. That doesn't matter. She's your wife and you know she's worth more to you than just her appearance. Who cares what she looks like so long as she survives? Will I be able to take care of her? What if she does die? I can't even fathom that. That's not going to happen. It can't, right? What if she doesn't know how much I really do love and care for her?

Steve begins sobbing at the prospect of possibly losing his wife forever.

"Mr. Smith?" Steve looks up at the nurse who's just burst through the doors of the waiting room. "We're done. Will you step in here please? We need to talk first."

SHIFT HAPPENS

Sometimes we choose the shift, and sometimes the shift chooses us. Sometimes we can be proactive about healing our unhealthy relationships and lessening our heightened anxiety by shifting our attitudes about ourselves, others, and the world around us. On other occasions, life-changing events force us to shift our perspectives.

> **Sometimes we choose the shift, and sometimes the shift chooses us.**

For instance, by reading this book or seeking professional counseling, you're actively choosing to shift your mind in order to achieve a higher quality of life. Conversely, when confronted with the brutal realities of life, we may be forced to reconcile the life we lead with the life we wish we could have had. At such particular junctures in our life, two wildly divergent paths form before us. One path demands humility and the will to change while the other path seeks to soothe the weary traveler with denial or further flights of fancy. **One path requires that we learn how to truly communicate with other people, while the other path allows us to keep living in the fictional worlds we've created in our heads.** One path leads to relational wellness, while the other path causes you to walk right by the same people you've always dismissed before.

For Steve and Lauren, the shift was forced upon them. Dealt a devastating blow in Lauren's sudden cancer diagnosis, both of them begin wondering if they ever truly connected with each other. Despite having been mostly happily married for decades, both Steve and Lauren had lingering doubts about whether they really knew each other. Because they were so unsure about their closest relationship, they would later wonder how well they knew their daughter, their own parents, their friends, and their coworkers. This uncertainty about their own relational health made them second-guess how they had been treating everyone they knew. If they had never truly learned how to open up to each other, how much did they tend to keep closed off from other people? Independently of each other, though occurring at the same time, Lauren and Steve realized that something drastic had to change within themselves. They both honestly loved each other and cared for their family and friends, but they knew that the stories they had been telling themselves about each other had prevented them from really connecting. Both pleaded for a second chance.

Whether the shift is forced upon us or we choose to shift ourselves, such a soul-level change must occur as the first step in rewriting the stories we tell ourselves. If we cannot see the promise of why we need to divest ourselves of these damaging scripts, then we'll never attempt to do away with them. As I've said before, the stories we're so adept at forming in our minds often present us with characters and situations that are much more compelling than what real life offers to us. Plus, it's much easier to control the people in our minds than it is the people in our actual world. But, directing the stories of our minds is ultimately detrimental to relational wholeness. It's a stopgap measure we subconsciously take in order to exert control over our otherwise chaotic lives.

> **Whether the shift is forced upon us or we choose to shift ourselves, such a soul-level change must occur as the first step in rewriting the stories we tell ourselves.**

THE PROMISES

By stepping off of your internal director's chair and learning how to discard your favorite scripts, you will enjoy a two-fold promise:

- Your relationships will be better, healthier, deeper, and more honest.

- Your anxiety will decrease.

Regardless of where you are in life—whether you're just starting college or just entering retirement—it's highly probable that you would like to experience these kinds of promises. What's more, you would likely rather choose the shift than have the shift choose you. Pain, if processed correctly, does bring growth, but if we can circumvent such suffering and yet still achieve the same ultimate results—better relationships and less anxiety—that's a goal we should strive to achieve. In learning how to notice and then dismiss the stories you tell yourself, you can achieve a level of relational wellbeing you may have assumed was always just outside of your grasp.

But doing so is not as easy as reading this book. **It takes dedicated mental, emotional, and even physical work in order to cement**

the strategies that I'll describe, into concrete habits that come to mind as easily as your scripts used to. While the words I use to describe these strategies are simple and anyone can implement them into their relationships, a person has to exercise a certain amount of vigilance and self-awareness in order to see the fruits of their personal labor come to fruition in their relationships. In other words, I'm not prescribing a one-time, cure-all pill to fix your anxiety and heal your relationships. What I am prescribing are strategies that have proven themselves effective in the lives of hundreds of my clients.

THE STARTING PROCESS FOR THE PROMISES

Later, we'll take an in-depth look at the particular strategies I suggest to my clients. For now, let's talk about the generalities of what it takes to discard the stories in our heads in favor of what real life presents to us. In order to receive the two-fold promise described above, you must:

- Notice that you're writing stories in your head *all the time.*

- Realize that you have relationships with real people and not the similar-sounding people in your head.

Is it that easy? To begin with, it is, but this can sometimes be a challenging step for a person to take. This holds especially true when we convince ourselves that we know someone as intimately as possible, like two people in a committed relationship. When two people have lived with each other for a long time, both of them likely have hundreds of scripts about the other from which they've been pulling stories from for decades. These stories glue themselves to the other person in such a deep and lasting way that they may greatly affect the way one person sees the other. When these internal stories collide with reality, conflict erupts. So, to notice that you're writing stories about your significant other and then to realize that you're relating more to the person in your head instead of the person looking back at you can be a daunting challenge.

But, it is a challenge that can be overcome. For instance, a husband who struggles with seeing his wife as nothing more than a materialistic money-lover must first look to see why he thinks that is so. He must free his wife from the limiting shackles that his narrow definition of her has placed around her. He must not think of her as an object to be manipulated or dismissed, but as a real person who has her own motivations, her own family of origin issues, and her own current struggles (for acceptance, for love, for relational wellbeing, etc.). In other words, he must learn to humanize her. Even if she was partly motivated by materialism to marry him, it's very likely not the top reason for their marriage, and definitely not the sole reason for it. If he has held onto the belief in his mind that she's only with him because he has money, then he has dehumanized her. By casting his wife in such a narrow role in the movie of his mind, viewing her through a myopic lens, he has relegated her to a bit part in the play of his life: the gold-digger waiting for him to die.

Does that sound like a healthy way to live with someone you profess to love?

If such a man visited my office looking for ways to resolve this issue, I would offer a shift in thinking and in action. First, learn specific ways to engage with your spouse. It can start simply, like exercising thoughtful curiosity when speaking with his wife.

Instead of automatically assuming that she's going to spend their money on frivolous items, he could casually inquire as to what she's going to do with her day. I would encourage him to go beyond content-related conversations and into process-related conversations, where they both relate how they felt about particular circumstances and not just facts about the circumstance itself. By being curious, the husband stands to learn more about his wife's apparent insatiable appetite for spending money.

In a similar vein, I would suggest the husband to suspend judgment about his wife's activities, at least for a season. For all he knows, she may be acting out through spending money because she feels too judged by her husband for other issues in their relationship. If she doesn't feel accepted in her own home, maybe she has been fulfilling that need by escaping into shopping. Note here that the husband's behavior influences the wife's and vice versa—a cycle that can be deadly to a relationship. When one person blames the other and the other person chooses to withdraw in some form, the relationship can decay. In this particular instance, the wife isn't a victim because of her husband's judgmental attitude—she's responsible for her own choices. She can't control whether her husband stays judgmental and refuses to truly listen to her side of the story, but she can control her response to him and how she is going to function in the relationship.

If the husband makes a choice to be less judgmental, his wife may invite him past her well-built defenses as well as he may learn new information about her. By pairing curiosity with a lack of judgment, the husband can learn how to relate to the real person in front of him and not just the character he created in his head years and years ago.

Noticing the stories we tell ourselves is much like the cliché of peeling an onion—layers abound. Once you notice that you've been telling yourself a false story about someone else, you may find another untrue story hidden just beneath the one you uncovered. But the fact that you notice that next story means that you are finally starting to see how the stories you've been telling yourself have been negatively affecting your relationships and heightening your anxiety. It's the first small step in a longer process.

> **Noticing the stories we tell ourselves is much like the cliché of peeling an onion—layers abound.**

Pause here and think about the one person you love most, or to whom you are most emotionally connected. Now, remember the last time that you two had an argument. Like a ready teakettle, conflict brings to a boil what has been simmering for so long. Conflict is often a noticeable indicator of a person's inner life. When someone's reached their tipping point, they may let loose with a tirade of unexpected words and actions, many of which can cause relational damage, sometimes even severing relationships forever. For these reasons, looking at moments of conflict in our own lives can help us learn much about ourselves.

Now that you're thinking about the last time you had a major conflict with a loved one:

- What was the argument about?

- What did you think about the other person before the argument? During the argument? After?

- Did your relationship suffer because of that argument? Or were you able to move past it?

- Can you think of a particular story you may have made up about the other person prior to the argument that might have influenced the conflict?

- Did you exercise curiosity and restrain your judgment in order to really hear the person across from you? Or were you only waiting for them to say what you had already scripted for them?

- Did your words or actions try to influence them to a particular outcome (favorable to you)?

- In essence, how did the story you had been telling yourself about the other person collide with the reality of your situation?

- Knowing what you know now, how would you have handled the argument differently?

These are challenging questions, but they cut directly to the point of this chapter. If we refuse to be proactive about our relationships, the shift will eventually be forced upon us. At some point in our lives, whether through disease, death, or dire circumstances, it's very likely that we will be confronted with the glaring difference of who we are and who we wish we could have been. Instead of waiting for that moment to arrive, we can be proactive about restoring health, wholeness, vulnerability, and trust to our relationships.

> **If we refuse to be proactive about our relationships, the shift will eventually be forced upon us.**

In other words, how do we combat the stories we tell ourselves? Do we try to fix ourselves—or others—or do we try to minimize our stories? Unfortunately, this isn't an issue that can be fixed once and for all, but the tools and strategies provided to you in the following chapters will help you learn how to manage and cope with the stories you tell yourself. Because we can't peer into another person's mind and we can't know whether they're really relaying the truth to us, we must rely on strategies rather than one-and-done solutions. My job is to help you turn down the volume and intensity of your stories so that they don't have as much of an opportunity to negatively affect your relationships.

But first, we must have a firm understanding of why our relationships—and especially with those closest to us—often cause us so much stress.

RELATIONSHIPS CAUSE STRESS

"Assumptions are the termites of relationships." | Henry Winkler

THE MAIN ORIGIN OF STRESS IN OUR LIVES

While our stress stems from many different places, from finances to jobs to health, the primary source of our stress is relationships. One of the main sources for our anxiety is our relationships. Even when we believe we're experiencing stress because of an event, the original source of that stress can often be traced back to a relationship problem. Why is this so often the case?

> **One of the main sources for our anxiety is our relationships.**

When I talk about our relationships causing us stress, I'm not saying that everyone else in our life is the cause of our stress. That's worth repeating—other people do not cause our stress. It's our relationships with other people that contributes to our stress. Making this distinction between the main sources of our stress is a fine and delicate issue, but it's necessary that such a differentiation is made. Conflict in relationships is inevitable, and it's this conflict—or the fear of such conflict—that increases our stress levels. Both parties in a relationship bring their own particular histories, hurts, and hang-ups with them, and both parties must be responsible adults in how they treat each other. Still, even in the healthiest of relationships, conflict will occur and anxiety levels will increase. People will behave in ways that frustrate us, but we will also behave in ways that frustrate others. In other words, the stress in our relationships does not stem solely from the other person, as if they're always in the wrong. Rather, this stress arrives because we are physical, emotional, relational human beings who are capable of great selfishness as well as great love. Furthermore, even when we are functioning at our best, as a healthy emotionally and relationally mature adult, with others— there will still be conflict.

> **Stress arrives because we are physical, emotional, relational human beings who are capable of great selfishness as well as great love.**

If you don't believe that relationships are the main source of stress, think about the last time you were by yourself for an extended period of time with no work to do, no deadlines to meet, and no expectations from clients or personal relationships. If your mind wasn't fixating on another person, how stressed were you in that moment? On occasion, when we're alone and able to set our own course, our stress level is less because other people's feelings and actions have little to no sway over what we want to do in that moment. For example, a mother of four with a rare day off from the kids may feel quite relaxed compared to the stress of her daily life where she's responsible for her children. Not to mention the other primary relationships in her life: her husband, her siblings and parents, her business relationships as well as her friendships. **With each new relational responsibility, the possibility for increased stress rises**.

Pause here for a moment and try to assess what percentage of your stress is directly tied to the relationships in your life. Is it 25% or 50% or 99%?

When you consider the top three areas of your life that are currently stressing you out the most, do you see faces in your mind before you recall experiences? Troubling experiences can oftentimes mask relational stress as well. In other words, the stress you may feel about a particular situation may actually have its origination in your relationship with a person involved in that situation. Think deeply for a moment about your current stress level and the people in your life to whom that stress may be attached. Rather than allowing this exercise to cause you further stress, try to take a cognitive, objective view of yourself and the relationships in your life that may be causing you anxiety right now. The point of this particular exercise is less about those specific people than about the reality that our relationships are oftentimes the greatest contributors to our stress levels.

EXAMPLES OF RELATIONAL STRESSORS

Let's take a quick look into the many different types of relationships that tend to be the most stressful.

If you have reared or are currently rearing a teenager perhaps you can identify with Steve and Lauren's constant battles with their sixteen-year-old daughter Emma. From spending too much time texting her friends to exercising her growing autonomy in dozens of disrespectful ways, Steve and Lauren's stress often centers on how they should be parenting their daughter. In addition to the stress each parent experiences during their frustrating encounters with a disengaged teen, Steve and Lauren also experience stress because of each other. Lauren thinks they should allow Emma a little more freedom while Steve believes their daughter needs to have more discipline. Because of their relationships with each other—Steve and Lauren, Emma and Steve, Lauren and Emma—every person in the family experiences stress as conflict inevitably occurs.

But relational stress does not only occur in our families (although it's often the most pronounced and most troubling origin of stress in our lives). **Anxiety in our lives also stems from the other people we spend the most amount of time with: our coworkers, bosses, or business partners.** In the crucible of a fast-paced, results-oriented, profits-based work environment, employee conflict can erupt at any moment. Take, for example, Steve in the story that began this book. One of his main points of anxiety while on vacation was about whether he was going to lose his job and whether or not his relationship with his boss was healthy enough to sustain downsizing. If we could peel back the internal curtains on Steve's stressors, we would also see how his fear of losing his job resulted in feeling anxious about his marriage. After all, if he had lost his job as the family's sole provider, what would Lauren think of him?

Beyond those we live and work with, anxiety comes into our lives by way of our friends and extended family members as well. Sometimes, because we don't see or talk to these people as often as we do those we see every day, our anxiety can increase because there's often so little we truly know about the troubling situation at hand. For instance, when two lifelong friends have a major falling out with each other, neither may speak to each other for months or even years. As time goes on, each person tells themselves a story about the other person, and it's within these falsified, fill-in-the-blank stories that each person's anxiety level increases as soon as they start thinking about the other person. This makes it increasingly difficult for either person to approach the other because of the immense amount of anxiety about the relationship that's been allowed to fester over time.

> **As time goes on, each person tells themselves a story about the other person, and it's within these falsified, fill-in-the-blank stories that each person's anxiety level increases as soon as they start thinking about the other person.**

Lastly, even relationships that exist on the relational periphery of our lives can cause us stress. For example, Emma's high school soccer coach chose her to play for the Varsity team even though she was only a sophomore. While she was ecstatic about it, her parents feared that she would be sacrificing more playing time on the Junior Varsity squad in exchange for the notoriety of riding the bench for the Varsity team. Steve and Lauren made their concerns known to the coach, and the coach promised them that Emma would definitely get playing time. As Steve and Lauren attended game after game just to watch their daughter cheer her team from the bench, they became more and more frustrated at the coach's decisions. Because of such a peripheral relationship that angers them, Steve and Lauren's stress levels increased with each game.

What's most telling about these various examples is that they tend to stack upon each other. It's not as if there's only one person in your life who may be causing you to feel more stress than others. More often than not, you will have multiple people in your life who contribute to your anxiety levels in different ways. Sometimes our anxiety has a way of spilling over into other parts of our lives and damaging other relationships. If you're an anxious, stressed-out person who has not learned how to calm yourself, many of your relationships may be suffering because you're unsure of your anxiety's main origin. In other words, your stress about a few particular relationships may be affecting every single one of your relationships without you noticing. For this reason, noticing and being aware of our stress levels and our anxiety's origin is imperative.

WHY DO RELATIONSHIPS CAUSE US STRESS?

Have you ever considered why, exactly, our relationships cause us stress? For the most part, the relationships to which we are most emotionally connected usually are the most stressful. Emotionally connected relationships come with more risk, require more vulnerability, and there is more to lose. We wouldn't feel so anxious about such a relationship if we didn't want to experience a healthy connection with them. On the other hand, and this is something we'll discuss in-depth in the next chapter, we often experience anxiety because we can't control the other person. In either instance, whether we seek relational health or our own selfish means, relationships cause us to feel stressed.

> **The relationships to which we are most emotionally connected usually are the most stressful.**

Part of our stress-inducing relationships involves our expectations of others. For instance, as we pointed out earlier, much of the early stories Lauren told herself about romance and love were influenced by Disney movies. Since most of the classic Disney movies resolved themselves at the point where the princess gets married, the audience never sees what happens after the wedding. Consequently, as a young girl Lauren was certain that once she found her Prince Charming, they would live happily ever after. However, Lauren and Steve had the first major argument of their marriage just a few days into their honeymoon. That singular event caused Lauren to wonder if that was going to be the norm for their relationship and not the long-lasting peace and contentment that she was sure awaited them as a married couple.

What I'm driving at is that we must expect to encounter conflict in our relationships. **When we live within the reality that conflict is likely to occur at some point in time in any of our relationships, we better prepare ourselves to handle**

that conflict in a meaningful, constructive, mature, and more adult way. Additionally, we lessen the stress we place upon ourselves in considering how to handle the various challenges in our relationships.

Put another way, many couples with unrealistic expectations of marriage believe their lives will be like sailing on smooth waters since they've found the one person who truly understands them. But when an inevitable storm arises (and most storms are out of your control), the person who expected still waters will be doubly anxious about surviving the event. The one most prepared to weather such a storm will have much lower, if any, stress levels. Storms will come, but we can prepare ourselves for them and even be stronger for the experience of having endured them.

Marriage may be the most challenging type of relationship in existence. In throwing two people together for a lifetime, neither spouse can truly hide from the other. While each spouse may have entered the marriage with their own protective barriers already built sky-high, over time each person in the relationship will discover the other person's weak spots, and perhaps even their own, whether by accident or on purpose. **Furthermore, a spouse is a mirror who shows us characteristics of ourselves we would rather not see reflected back to us on a daily basis.** As I've told clients before, we're all the healthiest people on our own, but as soon as we enter into an intimate and committed relationship with another person, all of our personal mess shows up with us. And remember that each person brings their own mess. When this happens, the relationship becomes, well, messy.

> **Marriage may be the most challenging type of relationship in existence.**

Therapist Daniel Wile says that "choosing a marriage partner is choosing a set of problems." There's truth in that statement. Whether you're more adept at identifying your spouse's problems than you are your own, you know that marriage can be rife with problems. It's not that Wile is miserable in his own marriage. Rather, he's offering a realistic portrayal of a committed relationship replete with what each person brings to the relationship in regards to their own humanity, hurts, history, and perspective. When two people with so many internal issues collide, external friction happens. Conflict erupts. Stress increases. And unless one or both parties does something about that anxiety, the relationship will suffer.

> **"Choosing a marriage partner is choosing a set of problems." — Daniel Wile**

Furthermore, a vast majority of this relational stress originates in the stories we tell ourselves about the other person. Based on my research, upwards of ninety percent of the stress in our relationships is due to the anxious, negative, expectation-filled stories that we tell ourselves about the other people in our lives. **When we ascribe made-up thoughts, feelings, or motivations to another person, we increase our own anxiety levels for *no good reason*.** We make ourselves miserable because we don't always know the full picture of the troubling situation. If we're not able to properly discuss or process the situation in due time, we'll experience low-level, misdirected anxiety that could turn into depression. Or, we could internalize much of that stress, effectively bottling it up, but when that happens, it's much more likely that we will emotionally react or explode at the other person once given the chance. I tell my clients daily that any time we internalize emotions, thoughts, or feelings, over time we will either "act in" or "act out." **We "act in" through anxiety and depression or "act out" through outbursts of anger, rage, addiction, or other escapist and numbing behaviors.** *Neither option is healthy.*

> **Based on my research, upwards of ninety percent of the stress in our relationships is due to the anxious, negative, expectation-filled stories that we tell ourselves about the other people in our lives.**

Much of life is lived between your ears. What we do in our minds makes a big difference on how we react or respond to those around us. As you've likely heard before, and as my dad routinely told me as I was growing up, "Life is ten percent what happens to you and ninety percent how you react to it." When we react to a negative situation or troubling relationship by fabricating stories in our mind that either make us feel better or make us feel like we're in control, we're actually doing more damage to ourselves than anyone else involved in the issue. We make ourselves miserable by telling ourselves ridiculous stories. **Life is ten percent what**

happens around us and to us and ninety percent the stories we tell ourselves.

So if our relationships cause stress, how do we rid ourselves of the latter without losing the former?

TOWARD LESS PERSONAL ANXIETY

"The greatest weapon against stress is our ability to choose one thought over another." | William James

THE TWO HIDDEN ISSUES OF FRUSTRATING RELATIONSHIPS

Now that we know the main origin of stress stems from our relationships, let's take a deeper look into why that is and what we can do about it. A large part of the reason that our relationships cause us stress is that we often want to change other people's behaviors. Because we are human, with our own unique histories, families of origins, past hurts, future dreams, and hidden desires, our basic behavior as humans leads to stress in our relationships. Put another way, when we tell ourselves stories about other people based on the many scripts we've pulled together from a wide variety of sources, more often than not, those scripts put our relationships at risk. The identifying characteristics of humans, i.e., the fact that we're both rational and emotional beings, is simultaneously the one thing that we have in common and the one thing that tends to drive us apart from each other.

> **A large part of the reason that our relationships cause us stress is that we often want to change other people's behaviors.**

We may say that we want healthier relationships, but we also interact with other people based off of scripts that we've already written for them. This is at the heart of the stress we allow into our lives. Stress mainly occurs because we want people in our lives to behave as we'd like them to and not as they actually do. This can reveal itself in a wide variety of ways and contexts, but if you drill down to the core of relational conflict, you'll likely discover that at least one person is trying to control the other in some way—even if the person trying to exert control doesn't recognize what they're doing in the moment.

Going back to the previous chapter, consider the three people you thought about that tend to lead to the most stress in your life. Your list could include your spouse, child, parent, friend, coworker, boss, or an extended family member. Beyond simply naming who those "stressful people" are, *take a few minutes and answer these questions:*

- Can you identify the particular actions or behaviors they commit that rile you to no end?

- What specifically do they do or say that gets under your skin in seconds flat?

It can't be overstated: A major part of resolving relational stress is simply noticing and being aware of where that stress originates. That involves identifying both the person and the specific behavior that person performs that seem to lead directly to your increased relational anxiety.

> **A major part of resolving relational stress is simply noticing and being aware of where that stress originates.**

When stressed about a relationship, a common word my clients use to describe their feelings about the situation is "frustrated." This is such a common term that we can sometimes dismiss it as just being "mild irritation" with another person, but frustration goes much deeper than that. I define frustration with two more "feeling" words: sadness and helplessness. A frustrated person is sad about the situation in general, but feels helpless to do anything specific about it. Being frustrated with a stressful relationship can be either positive or negative, yet both instances find their genesis in the hurt individual's desire to change the other person's behavior. What do I mean by that?

Consider a husband with an alcoholic wife. He may come to my office and say, "Her constant need for alcohol is ruining our relationship. I can see how her addiction is influencing the way she treats me, our kids, and even herself. If something doesn't change, I know something bad's going to happen." He may break down at this point and begin to cry, then confess, "I'm at my wit's end. I don't know what to do. I feel totally helpless."

Consider this wholly different situation. An accountant may come to my office complaining about her current job situation: "My manager continues to micromanage my performance. I need more freedom to do my job. I could be such a better worker if only they'd let me be and trust my work. My boss is driving me crazy. He's holding me back from getting the promotion I've been working so hard to get. But what am I going to do? I can't leave now. I just bought a house! I tried talking to him too, but I could tell that he wasn't really listening to me. I feel stuck."

In the first example, the husband wanted his wife to get help. Though he still wants to change her behavior, this is a positive example of seeking control. Because she is having a difficult time and can't help herself, he wants to help her, their kids, and himself. In the second example, the accountant wanted professional advancement. By itself, this isn't necessarily a negative example. However, her ego may be seeking to control her boss's behavior more than her capabilities may qualify her for a promotion. Because she can't get what she wants out of her job, she feels stuck.

Note that both of these individuals are frustrated with their relationships. They're saddened by the situation (for very different reasons), and they even use the words "helpless" and "stuck." When my clients use such words, I can surmise that their relational stress levels are on the rise. When I hear such terminology, I work to show them the vast difference between what they're expecting out of the other person and the true reality of their situation. In seeing the difference between the story in their head and the truth of real life, their stress levels begin to decrease as we work together to find mature, emotionally healthy ways to handle the situation.

Anxiety is a refusal to accept life the way that it is, rather than the way we want it to be. Both of these illustrations fill each affected person with anxiety, and so much so that it erodes their relationships. They either cannot see or cannot accept the vast difference between the stories they tell themselves and the harsh truth of their reality. Though the examples differ, both parties want to change the behavior they see in other people because that behavior adversely affects them. To reiterate, we experience stress because we want people in our lives to behave differently. We want our fantasy over their reality. We want them to behave as we assume they should behave and not like they're actually behaving. But, as you likely know from personal experience, changing someone else's behavior is a very challenging task.

> **Anxiety is a refusal to accept life the way that it is, rather than the way we want it to be.**

Before we go into the main reason why we want to change other people's behavior, I'd like you to consider one more point in regards to helplessness. The main reason most people curse, and especially those whose conversational artillery includes an abundance of F-bombs, is *helplessness*. Don't believe me? In English, "f—" is the most significant, verbal expression of anger. Anger itself is a "power emotion," something that we feel when we're totally helpless. For instance, the accountant from our earlier story might have referred to her manager as "that f—in' manager of mine." Because she has no real life control over his actions, she assumes control over him through her words. By using such strong language, she's mentally placing herself "one-up" against her manager because she feels like she's "one-down" to him in real life. She's mentally trying to reset the balance of power, even if only for a moment, so that it favors her rendition of reality and not what actually exists. While there are many words that we use and actions we take that work in this "one-up/one-down" way, assailing stressful relationships with F-bombs (out of the other person's earshot by the way) is one of the most common I hear.

But, it *is* important that I hear them. Within my professional capacity as a therapist, it's becoming easier for me to hear what's being said just below the surface of a conversation. But, with a little knowledge and practice, you can learn how to hear what a person really means when they're spouting off curse words and derogatory remarks left and right. We must learn to truly listen to others because it's through listening that we'll begin to understand why people use the words they do. We have a choice. We can either *judge* and *criticize* others or we can *observe* and *notice*. When we choose to observe and notice, we posture curiosity and look for the reasons why others choice certain behaviors. This process can be enlightening and can help us humanize the person. When we judge and criticize, we go "one up" making ourselves "better than," contributing to relational distance.

> **We have a choice. We can either *judge* and *criticize* others or we can *observe* and *notice*.**

WHY WE SEEK TO CONTROL OTHERS

Why do we spend so much mental time and effort on trying to control other people's behaviors? Because their real life actions may result in us experiencing emotions that we would rather not feel. Again, it's much easier to control the other person in our head than it is to control the other person in our reality. Because we can edit our scripts whenever we want to, we can ensure that their reactions to us don't hurt us. Because we fear experiencing pain similar to what we may have endured in the past, we erect defenses to protect ourselves. The stories we tell ourselves are a foundational part of our natural defense mechanisms. In fact, we can insulate ourselves so well with our internal scripts that we never seek to resolve a conflict with the real person. We consider the issue resolved in our own minds and move on with life, that is, until we meet that person months or years later and are brought face-to-face with the repercussions of our inaction. But that's tangential to what I'm driving at: we seek to control others because we desire safety for ourselves.

> **We seek to control others because we desire safety for ourselves.**

Every experience in life includes both an external and an internal experience of that moment. As much as our five senses help us make sense of any given situation, so too do our internal feelings. When receiving bad news like the death of a loved one, our bodies will physically tighten up and our stomachs may turn. Our breathing quickens, as does our pulse. There's a notable physical reaction to such news. Likewise, our feelings will change. And while we may not be able to describe that feeling in words, we know one thing for sure: I never want to feel this way again.

It's this final feeling—a combination of our external and internal reactions to a problematic situation—that causes us to want to control other people. Subconsciously, we're thinking along these lines: *If I don't want to feel this way again, I need to figure out a way so that other people can't make me feel this way again.* Both the body and the mind go into a fight-or-flight pattern, willing to engage or escape the conflict for the sole purpose of survival. We think, *If I can defeat this thing, then it won't hurt me,* or *If I can outrun this thing, then it won't get to me.* When it comes to our relationships, neither of these options works in the long run.

There are a number of fallacies at work in our fight-or-flight response to stressful relationships. The most glaring error is believing that other people cause us to feel a certain way. For instance, I've lost count of the number of times someone comes into my office, angry at another person over a particular event, and they use a phrase like, "Well, the way he made me feel was . . . " People don't make us feel. We have feelings that can arise out of relationships and circumstances, but other people do not force us to feel one way or the other. We own our feelings. In stressful relationships, our job is to calm those feelings. This is a delicate line, but it's such an important distinction to make that I'm going to say it again: **people don't make us feel; we are the only ones responsible for how we feel about any given situation.**

When we're angry with someone, our anger may appear to be wholly directed at the other person. However, with hindsight or therapy or both, we'll likely come to see that our anger was more about our own sadness, helplessness, and anxiety over the situation. Because we don't want to feel those particular feelings, we blame the other person for our problems. That's why the origin of stress in our lives can sometimes be so difficult to detect. We spend so much time and energy pointing away from ourselves that we fail to notice what's occurring within our own minds and bodies. All relationships require two people, and we must take ownership of our stake in the relationship. When we place more than our fair share of the blame onto the other person, we're projecting our own hurts on them so that we don't have to feel what we don't want to feel. It's much easier to cast blame elsewhere than to take responsibility for it.

> **We spend so much time and energy pointing away from ourselves that we fail to notice what's occurring within our own minds and bodies.**

During a recent session, an angry husband said to his wife, "You never meet my needs. Why is it that I have to beg for sex? That's just not normal. You're just like your mother, cold and aloof." His sharp words—which come from a place of helplessness to change the situation—are an attempt to control his wife. Criticism and judgment are defensive mechanisms to get another person to change their behavior. Unfortunately, they rarely have the desired result. He's effectively saying to his wife, "You're the problem in this relationship." He's reacting to an unmet need in his life and trying to place the blame for their relationship issues on her shoulders—without looking at himself. In other words, he's not asking her, "What can *I* do to help us become more intimate?"

As a therapist friend of mine once told me, another definition of anxiety is "the perception of not being loved." The husband told himself that his wife did not desire nor love him, because of her low desire for sexuality. This increased his anxiety and anger toward his wife. As future visits would reveal, the husband had difficulty looking within and continued to try to control his wife in a variety of ways. He cast his wife in an active role as the problem and himself in a passive role, seeing himself victim in the relationship. Eventually, his anger softened and he began to look at his role in their intimacy issues. The best part of him showed up and he started to rewrite the story in his head based on the reality of the relationship where both parties play active roles in contributing to their marriage issues. His choice to look within as well as shifting his thinking required great courage, humility and hard work. It was a joy to witness.

> **A definition of anxiety is the perception of not being loved.**

This leads to a vitally important notion in regards to our relationships: people who can't control themselves try to control other people. This belief cannot be overstated. When people feel absolutely helpless to change the way they feel on the inside, they will try to do everything they can to control what's happening on the outside. They want to control other people's behavior so that their relationship benefits them in some way, i.e., reduce anxiety, eliminate pain, or meet a deep need.

> **People who can't control themselves try to control other people.**

Such control occurs in a myriad of ways too, both passively and directly. For instance, many people are adept at passive-aggressive behavior, subtly trying to influence others in their lives through guilt, manipulation, or avoidance. On the other end of the spectrum, some people work to influence others through highly emotional means, like going into a rage if they don't get their way, calling people names, cursing, or even throwing things. No matter the exterior form that such manipulation takes, it begins with a person seeking safety and control, and, as a result, they attempt to control the behavior of others. When anxiety is high and helplessness is present, they will do anything in their power to stop feeling that way.

The question is, then, what's the healthy way to stop feeling that way?

7 STEPS TO CONTROL YOUR ANXIETY

First, I'll provide you with the steps, then I'll share a personal story where I practiced each step and was awarded with a much calmer presence in the midst of steadily rising stress levels.

1. Notice your body and emotions.

Take a moment to become aware of your heightened state of agitation. Is your breathing short or your heart pounding? Are you sweating or tense? What about your internal world? What words describe your emotions and feelings?

To change our state of being, we must take note of our present state. In acknowledging that you're stressed, you've taken the first step toward calming yourself.

2. Breathe deeply.

Take multiple deep breaths, relax your jaw, and place your tongue at the bottom of your mouth. (When anxious, our tongues have a tendency to go to the roof of the mouth.) For a few simple moments, try to clear your mind and focus solely on your breathing pattern. Continue this breathing exercise until you physically feel calmer and your heart rate decreases. In being aware of your breathing pattern, you're aligning your mind and body so that it can proceed to effectively consider the next steps in this process.

3. Connect with your environment.

When anxiety is severe, connect with your environment, along with focusing on your breathing. While continuing to take deep breaths, take a moment to notice the space that you are in. If you are in a room, focus your attention on the material items in the room: couch, table, picture, lamp, etc. If you are outdoors, notice your surroundings: tree, cloud, water, building, storefront, etc. Notice anything that helps you attach yourself to what is in front of you in the here and now. When we are anxious, we are disconnected from our bodies—meaning our brain is somewhere else (usually in the future) and our bodies are in the present.

4. Control what you can control.

In the grand scheme of life, there's very little that we can actually control. Still, we must learn to control what we can control, like our physical and emotional reactions to troubling circumstances. If possible, do something proactive in the moment to control a controllable: make that phone call, visit a family member, or finish an overdue project for work. For especially troubling issues, seek professional help. Where you see an effective and healthy means to a solution, give it proper consideration and act on it if the option seems wise.

5. Surrender to what you can't control.

This step is more challenging than the previous one. In your present circumstance, consider the many things that are outside of your control. Name each one and consider placing it in a mental storage unit, far away from your present thoughts. Because you can't control it, there's no need to give it any more awareness, time, or energy than naming it and removing it from your mind.

In addition to naming and dismissing what you can't control, people often look to their spiritual lives in order to surrender their illusion of control when anxiety rises. For me, when I have to surrender to life on life's terms, leaning on my faith has been a great way to let go of what I can't control.

6. Talk to yourself in a positive manner.

Through affirming self-talk, tell yourself that your life is more important than whatever you're going through in that moment. Make a firm decision to disallow what's out of your control from stealing your power, time, and emotional energy. Why work yourself into a frenzy trying to change something that can't be changed? Your main goal in talking to yourself in a positive manner is to remind yourself of the joys of your life and not to focus on what you feel you may be losing in a momentary, troubling circumstance.

This particular step reminds me of a seven-day vacation I once spent with my family where a thief from another continent stole from me for five straight days. That thief was a stressful business relationship of mine with whom I was extremely frustrated with at the time. While he didn't steal money from me, he stole my time. I was so preoccupied with that strained business relationship for most of that vacation that I was seldom with my family even though I was physically present with them all the time.

But, it wasn't their fault; I was the one granting him constant power over my present time. Had I reminded myself of the steps above as well as the current joys of my life during that vacation— uninterrupted time with my wife and fun with my family—I wouldn't have ceded so much mental and emotional power to someone that was 2,000 miles away.

7. Do something life-giving in the moment.

Once you've noticed, breathed, controlled, surrendered, and spoken to yourself in a positive way, make an intentional effort to do something life-giving. What do I mean by that? Well, what breathes life into you? This life-giving act doesn't have to be momentous. In fact, these acts are often much more mundane but still invigorating to your soul.

For many people, it could be as simple as listening to music. The spiritually minded may prefer praying or reading an inspirational text. Others may simply need to find that one friend to hang out with who they know will simply be there for them without questions or judgment. You may even consider making a list of the simple, emotionally healthy things you like to do that cause you to feel better about yourself. While some of these acts may be masked coping mechanisms, if used in moderation they can serve to help you calm yourself during problematic circumstances. For me, it is things like music, painting, prayer, conversation, reading, and working in the yard—to name a few.

8. Repeat Steps 1 through 7 as necessary.

If your anxiety has not decreased by the time that you've worked yourself through the seven steps described above, start over. Depending on the level of stress you may be experiencing, you may need to go through this seven-step strategy multiple times before you're aware of a noticeable change in both your physical and emotional states of being. Once you feel as though you're "level-headed" and your body and mind are in alignment, you're much better prepared to handle whatever circumstance or relationship awaits you next. You've successfully calmed your anxiety.

However, if you've cycled through these steps and your anxiety hasn't noticeably decreased, consider talking to a therapist. People process stress in different ways, and the various circumstances of life can lead to persistent anxiety or sudden anxiety attacks. When your stress level is high and persistent or you've caught yourself acting out in ways that surprise you or cause harm to the relationships in your life, speaking with a professional therapist may help you discern if more intense anxiety exists.

In closing, here's my true-life story and how I followed the steps above to calm myself. While our relationships often bring out the largest stress factors in our lives, the anxiety that we experience on a daily basis can stem from a wide variety of people and places, even from something as mundane—and maddening—as morning traffic.

My office is based in Plano, Texas, and my drive requires me to travel on the Dallas North Tollway. While the DNT is great for getting to Dallas quickly, it also becomes easily bottlenecked with just one accident. On one particular day, I had to meet a woman about twenty miles south of my office for a fundraising initiative. I wasn't looking forward to the meeting because of the time it was taking out of my already full schedule, but it was for a good cause, so I went.

As soon as I got onto the DNT, I knew it was a bad choice. As I inched along at a snail's pace, I saw exit ramp after exit ramp backed up with dozens of cars attempting to find a faster route. By the time I'd considered exiting myself, it was too late. I was stuck and the traffic wasn't moving. Seconds turned into minutes and minutes turned into what seemed like hours. I don't think I traveled more than fifty feet in thirty minutes—at least that's what it felt like. During that time, my stress levels increased to an unhealthy amount. Banging my hands on my wheel and yelling inappropriate things at other drivers (who were just as stuck as me), I suddenly realized how much I was letting something out of my control, control me.

So I decided to do something about it.

I noticed my physical reaction to the situation. My heart rate was accelerating, and my chest and stomach were tense. My fingers were gripping the wheel with unnecessary force. **I also became aware of my emotional response.** I was afraid that the person with whom I was meeting was going to be upset with my lateness. Because I didn't know her very well, I feared that she would think I was rude. I thought she might think I wasn't taking her fundraising endeavor seriously enough.

After realizing how much my body and mind were centered on things and people outside of my control, **I took a few deep breaths to gather my thoughts and emotions.** Once I felt better in both body and mind, I considered what I could control in the present circumstance. **I reminded myself, control what you can control and surrender what you can't.** I made the air conditioning blow colder, a simple act that helped both my physical state of being and my emotional health by making me believe, if only for a moment, that I did still have control over something.

Next, **I made a mental list of what I couldn't control in that situation**: the traffic itself, other people waiting in their cars, the car accident blocking the tollway, what time I would arrive at the meeting, the other person's response to my lateness, what would happen with our business relationship because of my lateness, how this setback would affect the rest of my day, etc. One by one, I named these uncontrollables and flung them away from my mind. I asserted mental power over them instead of allowing them to assert mental power over me. I refused to be further controlled by what I couldn't control. I surrendered, and in surrendering I found freedom.

Next, **I reminded myself that whatever you're going through right now is not as important as your life.** *While this traffic jam may cause relational stress in time, there's no need to worry about something that hasn't happened yet. It may not happen at all. If the* *person I'm about to meet knows Dallas, I'm sure she'll understand me being late because of traffic.* By giving credence to rational thought, I prevented my fears from overtaking my present and stealing more of my emotional energy. Through self-talk, I told myself to enjoy life in the now.

Lastly, **I did something that always breathes life into me**: I started listening to a podcast. With nowhere to go, and time to spare, I began playing a spiritual podcast that caused my mind to leave its agitated state and consider the higher issues in life. The hours I felt like I'd spent in the car soon turned back into minutes, even to the point where I was a bit upset that I didn't finish the podcast before arriving at my destination.

Because I'd followed those seven steps to calm myself, I wasn't stressed at all when I got to the meeting. Unfortunately, the person I was there to meet was frustrated by my tardiness. For a few minutes she let me know how I was negatively affecting her day and making her future appointments back up. I apologized, but never became upset or stressed because of her reaction. Because I had calmed myself, I could approach this small relational speed bump with grace.

Following those seven steps to reduce my anxiety helped me to rewrite the story surrounding my reality during that seemingly endless trip down the Dallas North Tollway. In calmly considering my situation, I was able to recognize where unnecessary stress was affecting me and how it might affect my relationships that day. I was reminded that reducing one's anxiety and practicing the art of being present is a matter of telling myself a story that adheres more closely to the facts of reality around me and not to the grand fantasies or worst nightmares we often seem so capable of creating when at our most stressed. When our minds live in the real world, our relationships can thrive.

What if all of our relationships—our marriages, our families, our friendships, and our business relationships—could thrive like that, even when the other person might be fuming?

TOWARD BETTER RELATIONSHIPS IN MARRIAGE, FRIENDSHIPS, AND BUSINESS

"Healthy intimate contact between people comes when one person shares his or her reality with the other, and the other comprehends it without judging or trying to change it." | Pia Mellody

BUILDING BETTER RELATIONSHIPS

Imagine a life where your most troubling relationships transform into healthy connections with other people. Peer into your near future and consider the very real possibility that your relationships can be more enjoyable, more fulfilling, more enriching, more productive, and more life-giving than they are currently. Even for people who deem their relationships to be healthy, there are areas in our lives that we can all work on in order to experience deeper connections. Furthermore, even healthy relationships experience the ups and downs of daily life. What if we could learn how to weather such storms? What if we could understand and implement what true relational connection requires?

For simplicity's sake, I've separated the various spheres of our life into three distinct areas: marriage and committed relationships, friendships, and business relationships. While we must approach each type of relationship in a different way, we can use similar strategies to seek true connection. For now, let's look at what we could expect in each type of relationship if we put into practice the strategies I've described thus far.

Imagine a marriage or committed relationship where neither person feels anxious or desires to control the relationship. They are good partners, a team committed to each other's best interests. They're able to handle their finances and their children well because they know how to communicate honestly without taking statements or disagreements personally. They are good friends who know how to have fun, when to work hard, and are supportive of each other. Lastly, they're intimate partners: they intentionally connect with each other through conversation, emotional vulnerability, and sexuality.

Now, **imagine a friendship that feels like family, where two people have connected with each other so well that the both of them can comfortably be together in silence for hours**. Because they've known each other for years and have been through some difficult times together, they've developed an inherent level of trust where each person knows that the other has their best interest at heart. They're a nonjudgmental sounding board for each other's gripes and opinions and only provide suggestions when asked. Plus, they know when to have fun so that the worries of the world can disappear from their lives for just a little while. Two men might feel as close as brothers; two women as close as sisters.

Lastly, **imagine a business relationship where each person brings out the best performance in the other.** Imagine a working relationship where greed or ambition is absent, where two people seek to genuinely help each other for the good of the company and not for self-gain. Imagine a workplace that these employees look forward to going to every day because they honestly enjoy what they do, the people they work with, and the meaning they find in their work.

Now, at this point you may be thinking: *I would love to have a spouse who always gets along with me, a friend like a sibling, and a boss like a mentor, but that's just not realistic. Have you met my wife? My husband? My boss?*

It is absolutely possible to have a better marriage, better friendships, and better business relationships, but the cost of such a reward is high because the vast majority of the work has to be done by you. I think this is why many people automatically shrink back from thinking their relationships could be any better. They may (consciously or subconsciously) know their shortcomings in the relationship and have no inclination toward working on themselves in order to make their relationships work.

Of course, I am under no illusion to believe that the strategies I outline in this book are the only thing that will "fix" your relationships. Mitigating, causative factors exist that can provide someone with a head start, so to speak, in having healthy relationships. For instance, when it comes to marriage and committed relationships, it helps to be deliberate and careful in choosing a partner. Picking someone to spend your life with who has a diametrically opposed worldview and approach to life has the potential to be a source of great relational stress. The same need to choose wisely also affects friendships and business relationships. Additionally, you can help your relationships by being proactive and intentional about creating the kind of relationship that you want. In other words, a "close" friendship requires intentionality and investing in the relationship. A healthy marriage requires daily, soul-level communication. A productive working relationship requires honesty about your own capabilities as well as a certain level of vulnerability with your peers and superiors.

Furthermore, healthy relationships can have a kick-start if one or both of the people in the relationship have had healthy relationships modeled for them in some form. In the same way that negative modeling (by primary caregivers, the media, etc.) affects the way that we handle ourselves as adults, positive modeling provides us with useful scripts for our relationships. In other words, if you had two parents that doted on you while still helping you mature, be thankful for such an increasingly rare phenomenon. Their positive modeling has allowed you, in some ways, to skip many of the issues that others must deal with in terms of how their history negatively affects their relationships.

Lastly, an ability to admit how little we actually control in life, including how very little we can actually control other people, is another contributing factor when it comes to healthy relationships. **Ridding ourselves of the illusion of control is a freeing experience, but it's often a mental process that we have to cycle through again and again when we begin to feel**

anxious. When we take ownership of the fact that we cannot completely control others or our circumstances, we make space in our thoughts and emotions to consider what we can control: ourselves, our feelings, and our reactions to others.

However, what's more important than any of these contributing factors is how you "show up" to the relationship. Every internal word you use to tell yourself a fabricated story about another person is like a brick you place on the wall around your heart. Over time, those stories become barriers to true relationships. When we "show up" to relationships with a barrier already erected around our innermost selves, the likelihood of true connection occurring is nil. But these stories are one of the few things we can control in our lives. In other words, you can control whether or not to keep piling bricks onto your emotional wall, or to pick them off one by one so that the other people in your life don't have to scale an insurmountable wall just to communicate with you.

Put another way, you control the remote for your stories. At any time, you can press pause on the stories you're telling yourself. After pausing these stories, you then have control over the intentionality of your relationships. You can initiate an information-seeking, nonjudgmental conversation with another person so that you're not filling in the blanks of your paused story. Beyond that, the way we have such conversations is integral to seeking relational health. The words we use, the way we physically and emotionally approach the other person, and the focused attention we provide to them are all significant ways we "show up" to our relationships. If we don't "show up" in healthy ways, every other contributing factor is rendered useless.

> **You control the remote for your stories.**

Although I've been focusing on the detrimental effects to our relationships because of the stories we tell ourselves, I'm under no illusion that ceasing such stories is the sole answer to our relational problems. It is not the only solution, but it is a solution that I've seen work time and again in my clients' lives as well as in my own. Reducing the stories you tell yourself about other people will lessen your stress while strengthening your relationships. It's not that the strategies I've outlined are a one-time cure-all. Rather, they're steps you can take so that the likelihood of deeper and more meaningful connections greatly increases. You will experience different and better relationships *because you're showing up to the relationship differently*. Again, it's about controlling what you can control, and in any relationship the only person you can control is you.

HOW TO ACHIEVE BETTER RELATIONSHIPS

We've previously discussed various ways to decrease our anxiety so that our relationships might flourish. Here's another way to look at how we reduce the amount of stories we tell ourselves in order to experience better relationships.

There are two simple components to achieving better relationships, and they involve our internal and external experiences. When I speak of internal experiences, I mean that which occurs in your mind and in your heart, i.e., your thoughts and feelings. This includes how you think about others and how you manage your own stress and anxiety. When I speak of external experiences, I mean what happens outside of your thoughts and emotions, like how you actually treat others. In other words, how does what you think and feel find its way into the world and actually affect your relationships? Do you treat others based on the stories in your head or on actual fact after having a genuine conversation with the other person?

Our Internal Experience

When we consider the internal component of achieving better relationships, you must think about how you think about others. You must learn how to notice when you're making up stories about the people in your life. When you become adept at this practice and essentially catch yourself in the act, you must then press pause on those stories before they may taint your relationships. **By pressing pause, you're preventing the story from solidifying into an errant belief about the other person.**

Let's recall the sequence discussed earlier on how our internal stories become external behavior that can damage our relationships:

- We MAKE UP a story in our minds about another person, filling in the blanks with scripts we've picked up from a wide variety of sources.

- Based on that story, we develop an OPINION about the other person's behavior.

- With no new information, that opinion cements itself into a BELIEF.

- That rock-solid, though unfounded, belief turns into particular BEHAVIORS toward the other person.

We've become so adept at telling ourselves stories that this sequence often happens in a split-second. Like our innate fight-or-flight instinct that kicks in during times of conflict and danger, the stories we tell ourselves are an immediate and subtle defense mechanism we use to protect ourselves. But the end result of these false stories is that we treat others poorly because we're relating to them as they exist in our minds and not as they exist in the real world.

Another aspect of our internal experience we must learn to manage in order to enhance our relationships is our own stress. This is especially important when you don't have all of the information in a given situation, because a lack of information often leads to increased anxiety levels. For proven strategies on calming yourself, refer to Chapter 11.

Our External Experience

The main external aspect that we can control in our relationships is how we actually treat others. In addition to the ways that we think about other people and reduce our anxiety, we must be aware of the actions we take in our relationships. By mentally pressing pause on the stories we tell ourselves, we make ourselves more open to the stories we hear from others. Within authentic conversations, we can learn how to practice openness, humility, vulnerability, and all of the other characteristics I describe at length in Chapter 15 on "Becoming a Person of Presence."

In regards to positive external actions you can take to seek relational health, initiating a conversation with the intention of honest information-seeking is paramount. There are few words more healing to a relationship than "I want to hear your side of the story." In practicing the strategies I describe in Chapter 14 on "The Art of Being Present," you will be able to quiet the stories in your mind so that you can truly hear what the other person is saying. Another beneficial, external action to take is to refrain from talking negatively about the other person. When we stay stuck in a place of thinking about what the other person "may do" or "has done," we make ourselves the victim, effectively ceding power to the other person over our emotions and minds. Instead of talking poorly about the other person, consider healthy ways to process the situation with a trusted third-party, whether a friend or a professional counselor/therapist. In both the processing and the troubling relationship itself, focus on seeking wisdom and information.

By controlling our internal and external responses to those around us, we can begin to "show up" differently to our relationships so that our relationships will be different and better.

DISCOVERING THE DIFFERENCE BETWEEN INTUITION AND IMAGINATION

Throughout this book, I've cast the stories we tell ourselves in a negative light. I've described them as fabrications that we tend to make up about the other people in our lives. I've said that we tell ourselves these stories as a way to cope with feelings we don't want to feel and to control people we can't control. By pressing pause on these stories, we increase our opportunities for meaningful connections with others.

But out of the hundreds of stories we tell ourselves on a daily basis, what if a few turn out to be true? What if our intuition, which still uses incomplete information to paint a fuller picture, is right? What if our greatest hopes or worst fears about another person are realized?

First, let's take a step back and consider how we might be able to tell the difference between our intuition and the stories we tell ourselves. Intuition is the ability to understand a situation immediately without assistance from conscious reasoning. Some people may call it a sixth sense or a heightened awareness about particular people or circumstances. Intuition may be considered as a kind of inner perception and has been called "real lucidity." The famed Swiss psychiatrist and psychotherapist Carl Jung defined intuition as "perception via the unconscious." In other words, our intuition and the stories we tell ourselves are often close bedfellows. So how can we differentiate between the two?

> **Intuition is the ability to understand a situation immediately without assistance from conscious reasoning.**

To distinguish our instincts from our fabricated stories, we must have an information-seeking conversation with the other person. We can't know whether our intuition is correct by ourselves. We have to involve the other person by purposefully seeking out their side of the story. What they reveal can confirm your intuition or silence the stories you tell yourself. Either way, even your correct intuition does not negate the need for proactively having hard conversations with the goal of seeking health in your relationships.

For example, I make my living by leaning on my instincts while talking with clients. I'm on a constant lookout for subtle cues and messages conveyed through body language, tone, what a client says, and what they often leave out. When I am at my professional best, my intuition will kick in when I notice something alluding to a particular stress point in a client's life. At that point, I intentionally make a statement to help them become aware of what I just noticed and then ask a question to confirm or deny if my intuition is correct. I may say something to the effect of, "I noticed your body language change when you just said that. You looked down and your shoulders dropped. Are you feeling shame about what you just shared with me?" Even though all the signs that I've been trained to spot are alerting me to the fact that the client is feeling shame, I still ask them about it to ensure that my intuition is correct. If they agree with my assessment, then we can proceed and dig deeper into their lives. If they disagree, they may be in denial of their own feelings, or I could be wrong. At that point, I'll ask the client to add to or edit what I just conveyed to them. Regardless of their answer, my goal is to connect with each client and ensure that I'm not living in my head and assigning issues to them that don't actually exist.

When we live from a centered place of being relational, we are constantly asking questions in order to seek more information, understanding, and clarity for any troubling or confusing situations. Where we have little information, we want to be like conversational archaeologists on a dig to uncover as much knowledge as possible with the goal of connection. We want to know others and be known ourselves. It goes back to one of our basic human desires: we all want to be known.

Suzanne Kaufman, a therapist friend of mine, says this so well in just seven words: "Listen to learn. Speak to be known."

> **"Listen to learn. Speak to be known." — Suzanne Kaufman**

WHAT IF THE STORIES WE TELL OURSELVES ... ARE TRUE?

"I know he's having an affair."

"I'm pretty sure she's been stealing money from our company."

"I think our thirteen-year-old daughter has been talking to some older teenage boys."

For the people thinking these thoughts, if their fears are realized, the stories they've been telling themselves could turn into real-world nightmares. From devastating issues like infidelity to illegal activities like embezzlement to concerning events like a child growing up too soon, sometimes the stories we tell ourselves turn out to be true. More often than not, such stories can be some of the most negative ones that we tell ourselves about other people. Why is this? Because many of these stories are based on our deepest fears. Once we've allowed such fears to infiltrate our minds and discolor our relationships, we may be too far gone into a cycle of withdrawal or conflict to see the other person in any other fashion than the way our minds have already defined them. When the worst our imaginations can conjure up becomes our reality, anxiety skyrockets.

In some instances, we can tell whether a story might be true about someone else based on how hard we fight against that story being the truth. In other words, it's like a classic soap opera plot where a wife with an unfaithful husband constantly questions herself for questioning his fidelity. Because he's in the wrong, he manipulates her to believe that this fear is about her own imagination. He turns the tables on her so as to divert attention away from his escapades. He gets away with it, for a while, but eventually too much damning evidence mounts and she finally discovers what she feared was happening. Unfortunately, this isn't just a made-for-TV plot. It happens in far too many real life marriages every day.

So what is someone to do when their worst fears become reality?

First, it is important to pay attention to the process that our bodies and emotions go through when we experience loss and pain. Elisabeth Kübler-Ross describes the process as the stages of grief: denial, anger, bargaining, depression, and acceptance. Part of being human means that we should expect to cycle through those stages as many times as it takes in order to have resolution to the pain of our grief or loss. It is imperative, in a season of pain and loss, to reach out to our support system when our worst fears become reality—rather than going through it alone. Additionally, consider talking with a trained licensed therapist to assist with the healing process. Furthermore, leaning on your own personal faith journeys in order to seek peace and comfort in the midst of struggle. As a person of faith, I find this to be of inestimable value when my own fears become reality.

Withdrawal is one of the greatest temptations a person who has been deeply hurt by someone else must resist. It's natural for a hurt person to lose trust in people in general when they've been deeply wounded. They fear that opening up to someone else may result in the same outcome and more pain in their lives—something that they cannot even bear to consider. But when hurt people do this, they're still telling themselves made-up stories about other people. They're filling in the blanks of their minds with the scripts from their prior, hurtful relationship. While such storytelling is almost impossible not to do in the immediate aftermath of a painful relationship, a wounded individual must learn how to pause those stories so that real healing can begin. If this section resonates with you, consider reading Chapter 8 again on "The Pain of the Past." To have better future relationships, we cannot allow past relationships to control our present thoughts and emotions. While healing from intense relational trauma takes time and should be processed without being rushed, the goal of healing is to keep making steady progress toward future emotional and relational wellness.

> **Withdrawal is one of the greatest temptations a person who has been deeply hurt by someone else must resist.**

For the less devastating stories we tell ourselves that end up being true, like the example of a daughter whose parents believe that she has been talking to boys too old for her, we must still go through the same process. It's imperative to seek more information, ask questions while truly listening, and then make an informed, nonjudgmental decision about the issue. If the issue turns out to be true, we must seek to control what we can control (i.e., having a conversation with your daughter to see if her behavior warrants consequences or discipline) and surrender to what we cannot control (i.e., realize that she's not a little girl anymore). We must learn to accept life on life's terms and not just the way we wish life could be.

WHAT IF THE STORIES OTHERS TELL US ... AREN'T TRUE?

Here's the reverse of everything we've discussed in this chapter so far. For much of this book, I've cast you as the narrator and chief architect of a fantastic though ego-driven story that paints the people around you in fairly negative tones. I certainly do not believe that this is always the case, as we can just as easily tell imaginative stories to ourselves that serve to idolize other people in our minds. While these types of stories bring about certain issues as well, it's more often the negative stories we tell ourselves about other people that cause our relationships to break down.

My work with couples, spouses, friends, and coworkers shows me that, more often than not, the mess of our relationships occurs because *both parties* are guilty of telling themselves false stories about the other person. But let's say that you've finished this book and have begun to notice the way you internally talk about other people in your life. Let's say that you're making a concerted effort to truly listen to the people in your life. Maybe you even feel secure enough that you are ready to talk to that one person you've dreaded talking to for ages. After finally building up the courage, you meet with that person and practice every single strategy outlined in this book, talking as openly and vulnerably as you can about the specific way they hurt you. Yet you have a nagging feeling that they're not opening up to you.

At this point, you have to decide whether to base your stories about them on facts or fear. Ask yourself, "Is what I believe about the other person right now based on the best information I have, or is it based in fear that they still don't accept me?" Become aware of whether or not your emotions and cognitive thought are in balance to where you are not overtaking the other in terms of swaying your opinion about that person. When a person does not seem to be relating to you well, you must decide how much power and energy you want to give to that person, both in the moment and in the minutes, days, and months after that moment. If you find yourself getting frustrated by their inability to connect, press pause on your stories until more information can be learned or the other person has a change of heart.

When other people make up stories about us, we must also still manage our own anxiety. For instance, Steve may go to his boss and say, "I keep hearing rumors about layoffs. Is that true?" The boss, worried about his own job and what the bad news could do to his stock, bluntly lies and says, "Nothing to worry about there, Steve." But Steve notices that his boss does not make eye contact. Steve can feel the mounting tension in the office as well. Even though Steve has tried to have an authentic, information-seeking conversation with his boss, he received a lie in reply. In this moment, it's even more paramount for Steve to calm his anxiety about his job and accept things as they are. This is where the proverbial rubber meets the road with the stories we tell ourselves: because we do not have all the information that we need and we likely aren't going to receive it, we must still exercise restraint in making up fanciful stories. A situation like the one I described above is one where Steve is forced to surrender because there's nothing he can control about the situation.

> **We are all solely responsible for our emotions and our reactions.**

Better relationships are imminently possible, whether it's your marriage, your family, your friendships, or your professional connections. Regardless of whether your stories become true or others' stories are false, you are still solely responsible for the only two things in life over which you have any control: your emotions and your reactions. By learning how to calm yourself and truly relate to other people, you can be the catalyst to create the kind of relationships you want.

SECTION FOUR: THE PRACTICE

"My relationships can be transformed?"

TOWARD MORE CONNECTION AND FULFILLMENT

*"If we only listened with the same passion
that we feel about being heard."* | Harriet Lerner

DEEPER CONNECTIONS, LASTING FULFILLMENT

If we know that relationships are one of the primary causes of stress in our lives, why do we go to the trouble of seeking them in the first place? Why not withdraw from each other, especially when conflict arises? Why not attack each other, especially if we feel justified? Why worry about our relationships at all?

Because nothing is as fulfilling in life than a deep connection with another person. Few things in life bring such lasting fulfillment as knowing others and being known by them. When we can shed our masks of pretense and offer our true selves to those in our lives, the stress of keeping up the charade fades away. Conflict and misunderstandings will still occur, but the sure foundation you've worked to establish in each of your relationships will hold firm so that any shifting ground beneath your feet won't ruin your relationships. True connection leads to solid relationships that can withstand nearly anything.

> **Nothing is as fulfilling in life than a deep connection with another person.**

Yet we sometimes shrink back from seeking such relationships because of the cost-benefit ratio involved. We know that romantic, familial, friendly, and business relationships can be stressful. Our relationships can require much work, especially if you want them to be healthy and maintain that health. If you take a step back from your relationships and consider what they cost you (i.e., what they take away from you) you might second-guess your need for relationships. You spend time, money, effort, emotions, words, stress, and sometimes heartache in order to have and maintain your relationships. From that vantage point, having even a simple relationship, like a coworker might with their boss, is a lot of work.

But few people seeking healthy relationships think that way. When they think about their friends, family, or loved ones, they don't often consider what having a relationship with that person costs them because the benefit of that relationship is of inestimable value. For whatever the person gives up in terms of time, effort, etc., they receive much more in return. In healthy relationships, both parties do the hard work of the relationship in order to keep it healthy.

If we don't believe that true connection with another person is a deep, soul-level need that must be met, why do people get married? Why do we seek out romantic relationships that can be just as troubling as they are rewarding? Why do television series tease the "will they or won't they" types of relationships for so long and then resolve those relationships in their finales by celebrating marriage? Why does most music center on love? Because we crave real connection with other humans. And when we cannot enjoy such connection in our realities, we can at least live vicariously through characters on TV and the lyrics we sing.

So the question is, then, how do we experience deeper connections in more of our relationships?

THE AUXANO APPROACH© TO COMMUNICATION

In order to increase your possibilities at having deeper connections in your life, seeking information is non-negotiable. **The goal of such nonjudgmental inquisitiveness is to see the other person as a human being.** That might sound simplistic, but what I mean by that is you must avoid seeing the other person as an enemy. When you approach another person as an enemy in an effort to seek information about a troubling issue between the two of you, your perspective on the problem is myopic at best in that you are solely focused on the other person's words, behaviors, feelings, or attitude. If you view them as your enemy, you may also be approaching them in an emotionally charged state, like anger, frustration, or irritation. In other words, you're centered on the story you've been telling yourself about them despite the fact that you don't have all the facts. When you do the hard work of truly seeing and relating to this other present person as a human being—someone with thoughts, motivations, and feelings of their own that you aren't privy to—you're working to proactively prevent yourself from casting them as your antagonist in the movie of your mind.

After fifteen years of practice and research, I created the Auxano Approach© to communication and relationships—a developmental approach to therapy that highlights how marriage and relationship(s) challenge us to grow ourselves up emotionally and relationally. Part of the Auxano Approach© to communication is the way you posture yourself so that you're intentional about mentally and emotionally "showing up" and approaching the other person with honesty, openness, and humility. It's a simple though effective four-step process:

Step 1: Observe and talk about what you just noticed.

In order to combat the stories you tell yourself, you must first notice that you're telling yourself a story about someone else. This requires a growing awareness of your thoughts, feelings, and emotions. Step 1 is a benign observation about the story you're telling yourself. You could say that you're repeating back to yourself what you just saw or noticed in a nonjudgmental, noncritical way. This step demands honesty, humility, and vulnerability.

Step 2: Invite the other person to hear the story you're telling yourself.

This is an act that requires both courage and vulnerability. Because you do not know how the other person might react, you must have self-confidence in your own thoughts and emotions in order to say what you're truly thinking and feeling. Clients who employ the Auxano Approach© to communication are encouraged to use phrases like:

- "The story I'm telling myself is … "

- "The picture in my head is … "

- "The way that I hear that is … "

By using these simple phrases, one person pulls back the curtain on the movies in their minds in order to let the other person know what they are believing about that person in that moment. These are revealing statements and could initiate further conflict in the relationship, but they are necessary words to speak in order to see the relationship grow and thrive. Plus, when one party offers sincere words in a vulnerable manner, it creates an atmosphere of openness, which increases the possibility of connection.

Step 3: Share with the other person the feelings you have as a result of the story you made up in your mind.

After sharing the story they've been telling themselves, people may say something like, "Based on that narrative in my mind, I feel sad (or angry, hurt, frustrated, etc.)." This can be an even more intense step than the first because the person must reveal his or her heart, emotions, and feelings. If we only share the story we've been telling ourselves, we leave out half of the relevant information as to *why* we're sharing that story. In order to seek true connections and relational wholeness, we have to share both the belief that we have created in that moment about the other person as well as how that belief is affecting us internally. This can be daunting because while we may feel slightly uncomfortable telling someone else what we've actually been thinking about them lately, it can be more challenging to share how our true or false beliefs have led us to feel a particular way. But, like I said before, the cost-to-benefit ratio of your relationships is well worth the momentary discomfort you may feel in sharing your honest emotions with another person.

Step 4: Seek more information.

In this step, people use questions like, "Is that what you meant?" or "Did I understand that correctly?" It's of the utmost importance that the questioner now becomes an intense listener, pausing their stories about the other person and suspending their own thoughts and emotions for the moment. Brené Brown calls this "passionate listening." It's the ability to tune out both external and internal distractions, most notably the stories we tell ourselves, in order to focus on what the other person is *really* saying.

An intentional listener refrains from thinking about their own response while the other person's still speaking. How do you know when you've accomplished this task? Again, Brené Brown provides wise counsel: "When I really listen rather than thinking and formulating my response as people are talking, the entire conversation takes on a new cadence. It's slower and there's more white space between exchanges. It's a little weird at first, but it's also very powerful."

When seeking clarifying information, it's important for both the listener and the speaker to adopt their respective, respectful roles. The listener ought to suspend their thoughts while the speaker talks. One way I encourage my clients to do this is to visualize placing their thoughts on a shelf for a few minutes. They'll know where to find them later, but for the moment, they need to be somewhere just out of reach. The listener should listen with interest and seek to truly understand what the speaker is saying.

Furthermore, **a "sliver of space" must exist between the listener and the speaker.** This sliver represents the separateness of the two individuals in the relationship, but it also serves as a reminder for the listener to let the speaker have and express their own feelings *without taking on the other person's emotions.* In other words, if the speaker begins to get angry while sharing their emotions, the listener should allow for a "sliver of space" between them so that the listener doesn't likewise become angry. If the listener becomes angry during their exchange, that emotion will overwhelm their ability to truly listen to what the speaker is saying.

On the other end of the relationship, the speaker should work at verbalizing what I mentioned in Step 3, i.e., how they're feeling. The speaker should share what the experience was like for him or her by using "feeling" words—mad, sad, guilt, shame, etc.— and not sharing his or her perspective, opinions, or beliefs. If the speaker begins to share his or her perspective, opinions, or belief, he or she should try beginning statements with, "After hearing you say that, what I'm telling myself now is …"

As you can see, the Auxano Approach© to communication works most effectively when both parties in the relationship show up with openness and humility and can stand on their own two feet. This means that they can calm their own emotions without relying on the other person to do it for them. When both parties decide to show up to the relationship with the goal of moving it toward a healthy place, this is where the relationship sees its best chance for true connection. Plus, when the "best version" of each person shows up, meaning that they're able to calm their own anger and anxiety while also posturing humility and openness, they become attractive to each other. People want to connect with people who want to connect.

Recall what therapist Suzanne Kaufman says: **"Listen to learn. Speak to be known."** When each person in a relationship can remember—and act upon—these two short phrases, our opportunities for true connection increase exponentially. The phrases themselves are simple so we can remember them, but the power behind those few words lies within our ability to make them real in our lives. When we honestly listen to other people in order to learn their take on an issue at hand, as well as their feelings about that issue, we will see them as a human being and not just as an extra in our self-centered movies. When we speak to be known, with vulnerability, openness, and honesty as well as with boundaries—we show ourselves to be human beings and give the best chance for the relationship to succeed. The ideal is when both parties listen to learn and speak to be known, deep, lasting, strong connections have a much higher possibility of developing.

The four-step Auxano Approach© to communication accomplishes four distinct goals in addition to its overarching goal of helping you to establish and maintain healthy relationships:

1. It assists you in suspending defensive behavior.

This approach helps prevent you from erecting walls around your heart and mind because you're challenged to share from the core of who you are, through both your thoughts and your emotions. Defensive behaviors like judgment, criticism, aggression, manipulation, control, and avoidance are suspended from thought and action for the health of the relationship.

> **Defensive behaviors like judgment, criticism, aggression, manipulation, control, and avoidance are suspended from thought and action for the health of the relationship.**

2. It creates an environment to really know another person.

In practicing the art of being present, then becoming a person of presence, we learn how to focus on the present instead of the future or the past. When we become that focused on a relationship, especially one that may be causing us stress, and we know how to quiet our minds so we can truly listen to the other person, we begin to learn things about that person that will change the calcified belief that we had about them.

In other words, when we're able to press pause on the stories we tell ourselves and let the real life person speak, instead of hearing only the person's voice through the made-up characters in our minds, the other person becomes much more real to us. As a result, people that we engage no longer live in our head under our mind's dictatorship. Rather, they become people with their own past hurts, current struggles, and future worries. They may have family of origin issues just like us, or stake too much of their relational happiness on what they see modeled for them on TV. But in learning about the true beliefs, thoughts, and feelings of another human being, we find soul-level points of connection.

> When we're able to press pause on the stories we tell ourselves and let the real life person speak, the other person becomes much more real to us.

3. It creates an environment to be seen and known by another person.

By sharing the unvarnished truth of both your internal and external experience, you're welcoming another person into a space in your life that few others may visit. In being open yourself, you clear a relational pathway for the other person to be open as well. When both people are able to discard the pretenses and facades that all of us are capable of creating and maintaining, the opportunity for truly knowing another person increases. When we shed our masks through better listening and honest speaking, we will be known and know others. Such knowing and being known is something we silently crave. When we're able to verbalize our thoughts and feelings, especially if those thoughts and feelings are attached to a stress-inducing issue or relationship, we let others know us on a much deeper level. **Such vulnerability requires confidence to stand up for oneself, but it's a small price to pay for relational depth that could lead to lasting fulfillment.**

To know and be known is one of the main goals of committed relationships. We truly know another person and they likewise know us, we feel fulfilled in that relationship. There exists a sense of peace within your life, a stress-free place where your soul can rest. Conflict and misunderstandings will still occur, but by applying steps from the Auxano Approach© to communication and relationships at hand, your relationships can weather such storms so that they grow stronger over time instead of sinking in rough waters.

> **By sharing the unvarnished truth of both your internal and external experience, you're welcoming another person into a space in your life that few others may visit.**

4. It assists you in "standing on your own two feet" by calming your anger and anxiety.

The phrase "standing on your own two feet" can be taken both literally and metaphorically. It means occupying your own space in the world, firmly planting your feet on the ground as a sign of self-confidence and independence. Within relationships, it means staying separate from the other person in healthy ways. Consider the "sliver of space" illustration previously discussed. One who "stands on their own two feet" refuses to take on the emotions or feelings of the other person, especially during stressful situations.

Self-confident people with healthy boundaries will notice what's occurring right in front of them, but they will not absorb it or give it too much power over their thoughts and emotions. Even in the midst of trying circumstances, they should strive to balance their heart and their mind, ensuring that their internal and external boundaries are clear to both themselves and the other person.

The key here is avoiding reactivity. By avoiding knee-jerk reactions to a stress-heightened situation, people can take ownership of their own thoughts, feelings, and decisions. Choosing to not be reactive is less about words and communication than it is about how you posture yourself and show up to the relationship. What I mean by "how you posture yourself" is staying in your "functioning adult" state and not getting sucked into the "one up/one down" power moves. In addition, it means being vulnerable and talking about what the situation or conflict is like for you—resisting the urge of pointing your finger at the other. Someone "standing on their own two feet" will be a calm and assured presence who desires to see the relationship become healthy again.

> **Choosing to not be reactive is less about words and communication than it is about how you posture yourself and show up to the relationship.**

EXAMPLES OF THE AUXANO APPROACH© TO COMMUNICATION

What does the Auxano Approach© to communication and relationships look like in real life? Let's take a look at Steve and Lauren's arguments over their parenting styles, a common issue for parents of all ages. Give particular notice to the words that Lauren uses when replying to Steve.

> While Emma's at soccer practice, Steve and Lauren eat a mostly silent dinner until Steve suddenly says,
>
> "I can't believe you grounded her for a week from driving anywhere. You know how many activities she has these days. Now we have to take her everywhere. Why were

you so hard on her for being on her phone a bit too much lately?"

"Steve, when I hear you ask why I was being so hard on her, what I tell myself is that I'm not parenting well . . . that I must not be a good parent in your eyes. What that stirs up in me is anger, frustration, and sadness. I don't know if you've noticed, but my experience has been that my parenting has come into question a lot lately. Before I run to these assumptions about how I parent, I want to make sure what you actually mean when you constantly bring these things up. If I'm misunderstanding you, then I don't want to go down that path and develop loyalty to the wrong opinion. So help me understand your side. Is that what you really mean when you question my parenting?"

Steve replies, "No, that's not what I mean. You're a great parent. Sometimes you don't make the choices I would, but that doesn't mean you're a bad parent. I'd just like to know why you took away her car when you knew that would negatively affect all of us."

For the next few minutes, Steve and Lauren discuss Steve's subtle condescension when it comes to his wife's parenting skills, what feelings this stirs up for Lauren, and then discover common ground in the fact that they both want what's best for their daughter. But the stories they each have of what it means to be a parent differ in both large and small ways. As they uncover the many definitions of what it means to be a parent, Steve and Lauren draw closer to each other and eventually land on a workable solution to the problem Steve brought up in the first place. By listening to learn and speaking to be known, their relationship survives a small conflict that, without noticing it, naming it, and communicating with each other about it, could have turned into a latent, deep-seated issue driving a constant wedge into their marriage.

Because the Auxano Approach© to communication and relationships doesn't just apply to marriages and committed relationships, let's look at how it could be applied in a less intimate setting, such as a business relationship.

For nine months, Steve's been courting a big account for his company. Landing such a huge client would mean a heftier bonus, money that could help offset Emma's forthcoming college expenses. Without that bonus, he'll have to tell Emma to get a student loan or even consider moving home for a few semesters. In other words, Steve's pinning his financial hopes on his ability to reel in this big account. When he thinks that the prospective client may slip away, his stress level rises, but he dismisses the possibility of such an outcome because he doesn't want to consider what such a lost opportunity would actually mean for his family.

As the new client draws closer to signing the final contract with his company, Steve counts up the days that he hasn't heard from the client. *Has it really been seven days without a word? Didn't I email them just last week to make sure things were headed in the right direction?* As far as he can recall, Steve remembers the client say that she would get back to him in a day or two in order to review the final contract, but that hasn't happened yet. *So what's going on?* Steve wonders. With each passing day without a word from the client, Steve's anxiety level noticeably increases. He's in a nearly constant state of agitation and gets easily provoked by the most innocent of questions, especially when he's at home.

Over the weekend, the stories he tells himself are many and condemning: *I've put all my eggs in one basket with this client. If this doesn't work out, just think of all the months of work I've wasted. I'm going to have to start over and begin new relationships with potential clients. If I can't pay for Emma's college, what will Lauren think? How will Emma react? I'll be a failure in their eyes. And I want to avoid Emma having to get a loan or move home. She's two years in and loves it there. She's in a sorority, making good grades, and has a great support network of friends. How could I ask her to leave that and go into debt because her father cannot support her like he's supposed to? She'll never forgive me.*

When Steve realizes that he's telling himself stories about events that haven't happened *and may never happen,* he decides to put into practice what he and Lauren have been learning through counseling. He chooses to be intentional about this business relationship in order to fill in the blanks that are currently terrorizing his thoughts. Once he's back in the office, he calls the new client. It's the first thing he does that Monday morning. Without being pushy or seeming desperate, Steve gathers his thoughts, pauses his stories, and calmly tells his prospective client, "Just checking in to see where we are with the contract and if there were any questions I could answer for you."

He breathes a sigh of relief as the client replies, "So glad you called Steve, and I'm sorry it's taken longer than usual for us to get this done. Our legal team had to look it over, and one of our lawyers was on vacation, and, well, you know how these things go sometimes." Steve laughs a little to himself, "I do. I just wanted to ensure that I wasn't making up stories about why the process was taking longer than expected. I wanted to get the facts from you just to make sure we're all still on the same page." The client replied, "We're definitely on the same page, Steve, and we're looking forward to working with your company."

There's a noticeable difference in this relationship compared to Steve and Lauren's marriage. **In business relationships, you must adapt the steps of the Auxano Approach© to communication mentioned earlier because this is not a personal relationship. The level of vulnerability required is not as high as in committed, romantic relationships.** Consequently, steps 1, 2, and 3 (observe, invite, and share) may not be necessary and could be awkward to share in a professional setting. However, you can still internally process steps 1, 2, and 3 by mentally noting, or even writing down, the stories you're telling yourself and how those stories make you feel. Once you grasp that information, you'll be able to perform step 4 with precision.

In our preceding example, it would appear that Steve skipped directly to step 4, "seek clarifying information," but you should also notice that he internally processed steps 1, 2, and 3. However, long term or close-knit coworkers and employee/employer relationships may have a level of connection that allows room for deeper sharing to the extent that outwardly progressing through all three steps would be beneficial and recommended. But for most of our work-related relationships, proceeding to step 4 in order to gather more information is recommended as it helps to prevent us from rushing to judgment and making ourselves miserable in the process.

The next time you desire to seek deeper connections in your relationships, whether in your marriage or committed relationship, with a family member or friend, or with a coworker or boss, remember the four-step Auxano Approach© to communication:

- **Step 1: Observe and talk about what you just noticed.**

- **Step 2: Invite the other person to hear the story you're telling yourself.**

- **Step 3: Share with the other person what feelings get stirred up for you as a result of this narrative in your head.**

- **Step 4: Seek more (clarifying) information.**

Another way to recall these steps is to fill in the blanks of the following phrase with what's relevant to your situation:

"When you did _____, what I told myself was _____, and as a result of what I told myself, I felt _____. Can you tell me more about _____?"

Depending on the type of relationships and the issues that you may be dealing with, you may need to cycle through these steps before the stories in your head give way to the reality of your relationships.

Remember that the ultimate goal of these steps is not to gain control over the relationship, but rather to see, hear, and understand the other person as a human being just like yourself, one with their own thoughts, feelings, and motivations. When two people are able to get over themselves, press pause on their inner stories, truly listen to each other, and speak from a place of vulnerability, their relationship cannot help but to thrive. When you put this approach into practice across the full spectrum of your relationships, your relationships will experience deeper connections and you will begin to feel a sense of fulfillment in those relationships.

> **The ultimate goal of these steps is not to gain control over the relationship, but rather to see, hear, and understand the other person as a human being just like yourself, one with their own thoughts, feelings, and motivations.**

But being able to consciously, intentionally, and consistently put these strategies into practice requires the art of being present, a habit you can learn and one that becomes second-nature the more you practice it.

THE ART OF BEING PRESENT

"It is a mark of soulfulness to be present in the here and now. When we are present, we are not fabricating inner movies. We are seeing what is before us." | John Bradshaw

INTENSE INTENTIONALITY

In the spring of 2010, Serbian-born performance artist Marina Abramovic created an art exhibition at New York's Museum of Modern Art that showcased the piercing art of being present. For seven hours a day and six days a week, without food or water, Abramovic sat alone in an expansive MoMA gallery. One by one, museum visitors sat in the only other chair in the room, one that happened to be facing the artist.

Speaking was prohibited. Abramovic's installation centered on the simple though often overlooked connection made solely through eye contact. There were no stories to tell, no objects to hide behind, and no words to use to deflect from self—just the participant and the artist sitting across from one another, looking into each other's eyes. Some visitors sat across from her for a minute while others chose to be present with her for several hours. This resulted in countless meaningful connections between the artist and certain participants, leading to emotional responses like laughter and tears. Over the three months that Abramovic was there, 1,400 visitors sat in the chair.

Compared to the popular entertainment of our day, how did such a seemingly boring performance art piece attract so many visitors? How did it captivate so many that they lingered for longer than a commercial break? How did such a stark, bare-bones experience compel people to try it and then tell others about it? There are many answers to these questions, but I believe the attraction of Abramovic's performance art installation can be described in a simple way.

Along with our need for individuality and separateness, our need for connection is one of the greatest needs we have as human beings. When we live most of our days without truly connecting with someone else, there's something within us that yearns for real connection. Because everything else that so often distracts was stripped away, the museum visitors were able to make a true connection with another person. And this connection happened despite awkward silences and the fact that the other person was a total stranger.

> **Along with our need for individuality and separateness, our need for connection is one of the greatest needs we have as human beings.**

Abramovic may be gifted when it comes to the art of being present, but you can become a skilled "present artist" if you keep reading. Taking Abramovic's lead, learning to be present often starts with the eyes.

THE EYES HAVE IT

When's the last time you made prolonged, steady, and comfortable eye contact with a loved one? For some of us, this can be a challenge. Additionally, many people may think that they are making eye contact with another person when they are actually looking *just below* someone's eyes. Regardless of the context of the next conversation you have with your spouse, a family member, or a friend, become aware of whether or not you're making eye contact. If you're not looking the other person in the eye, force yourself to do so. It will be awkward at first, and you may even receive a strange look in return. But the more often you make steady, easy eye contact a habit in your life, the less awkward it will make you feel. If someone asks you why you're staring at them, be forthcoming and say, "I'm working on being more present in my relationships, and I've noticed that I don't often make good eye contact."

Furthermore, maintaining eye contact is a great way to assess whether or not you're maintaining focus on what the other person is actually saying to you. When your eyes wander away from theirs, it's probable that your mind is considering something wholly different than what's actually going on in your present situation. Whether you're thinking about what you want to say, what you want the other person to say, or something completely tangential to the discussion at hand, your wandering eyes often betray your intentions to be fully present. The next time you notice that your eyes have wandered from the other person, make a mental note of what you were thinking when that occurred. Then, resume eye contact with the other person and reorient your mind to what they're actually saying. In other words, the physical act of resetting your eye contact on the other person can be a mental reminder for you to refocus on their words.

> **Maintaining eye contact is a great way to assess whether or not you're maintaining focus on what the other person is actually saying to you.**

BEING PRESENT MEANS SHOWING UP

Eye contact is often the first step in making a meaningful connection with another person. It's a simple strategy that can help you be present with someone else so that you're sincerely showing up emotionally and mentally by turning all of your thoughts and feelings to the present moment. Often, we make the mistake of thinking that deep, meaningful conversations about fears, dreams, and our innermost thoughts are the primary way to connect in relationships. I have developed loyalty to the opinion that growing your ability to really look into the eyes of another person and truly "show up" emotionally and mentally is just as essential.

> **Eye contact is often the first step in making a meaningful connection with another person.**

When we really look another person in the eyes, it is common for us to have an internal experience—an emotional and physiological response that takes place within. The act of looking into each other's eyes by itself does not bring about a meaningful connection; you must have an added awareness of your own physical and emotional responses (peace, anxiety, sadness, increased heart rate, etc.). If we are willing to notice and listen, these responses can teach us about what we feel inside and how we feel toward the other person. This is one reason that we don't practice "exchanging emotional energy" by looking eye-to-eye with others on a regular basis: being present demands that we take an honest look at ourselves and the feelings—whether positive or negative—that we have toward the other person.

> **When we really look another person in the eyes, it is common for us to have an internal experience— an emotional and physiological response that takes place within.**

So, in addition to noticing where your eyes go during a conversation, also take a mental snapshot of your internal experience (physical and emotional responses) when you're actively pursuing "being present" with another person. What emotions or feelings do you feel as they share? Are you sweating, laughing, nervous, or excited? Is your heartbeat calm or steadily rising? What tone of voice are you using? Do you feel understood? You may even consider sharing these thoughts with the other person at an appropriate time.

By being honest and vulnerable about our internal responses with both ourselves and our relationships, we're paving the way for true connection. One of the greatest joys we have as human beings is to make a meaningful connection with another person—a friend, spouse, or our children. By making a meaningful connection, I mean that we are in the present with the other person and really show up, both emotionally and mentally. This type of intentional, significant connection is a gift you can give another person. It's also satisfying and rewarding for you.

> **By being honest and vulnerable about our internal responses with both ourselves and our relationships, we're paving the way for true connection.**

True connection with others gives significant meaning to our lives. I believe there's absolutely no substitute for making a significant connection with another human being. **Life itself lives in the exchange between two people**. Unfortunately, it can be difficult to make that kind of deep human connection, and many people try to substitute all kinds of things—work, hobbies, addictions—or make other unsatisfying attempts in order to fill that need. Other people avoid making a connection by talking in circles, generalities, or by deflecting. As a result, their lives are a smattering of surface conversations, going through life not truly knowing others or being known themselves.

> **True connection with others gives significant meaning to our lives.**

ARE YOU AWARE OF YOUR AWARENESS?

Making eye contact is a simple step within the much greater strategy of being present. Eye contact heightens your awareness of the other person as a real person and not just the person in your head that your stories keep telling yourself that they are. But the only way to get better at eye contact is to be aware that you're not very good at eye contact in the first place. Through the simple act of noticing where you might be relationally deficient, you can begin to take certain steps that will help strengthen your relationships.

In my sessions with my clients, I encourage them to assess their conversations based on two types of awareness: **external and internal**.

- **External awareness** means focusing on your surrounding environment, i.e., what's going on outside of your physical body.

- **Internal awareness** means focusing on what's going on within you, i.e., your mental, emotional, or physical reaction to the present situation.

Both types of awareness are supremely important to the art of being present, but people are often like a lopsided scale, heavily weighted down on one extreme or the other. In other words, a person may be highly attuned to their physical surroundings, but have grave difficulty in assessing their internal world. Conversely, someone else may be familiar with their internal realm, yet they're unaware about the physical world around them. It's important to relational health that an individual finds balance between these two types of awareness. To truly be present with another person, we must learn how to be equally aware of both our external and internal stimuli.

For those who've never considered what it means to essentially look at yourself while you're trying to connect with another person, developing the skill of awareness can be a challenging task. However, I can't overstate how important the simple aspect of awareness is to future relational health. By noticing what may be askew in your external or internal world, you're naming problems that can be fixed over time.

> **I can't overstate how important the simple aspect of awareness is to future relational health.**

Developing awareness is akin to strengthening a muscle. The more you "work out" the skill of awareness, the more adept you'll become at noticing even the smallest of details in your relationships. Additionally, the mental and emotional muscle memory of awareness will result in your ability to practice awareness *in the moment*. What do I mean by this?

I often talk to my clients about a **continuum of awareness**:

Continuum of Awareness

When a concerning event happens to us that brings discord to a relationship, we can still choose to exercise awareness of that event at any point after the event has happened. If it's a deep wound, exercising effective awareness may not happen until months or years later. As a person becomes more comfortable with noticing their own actions, motivations, and stimuli within a situation, their awareness may occur several days after the event. The more that a person exercises such self-awareness about their troubling issues, the less time they'll require after the event to properly process the situation. In time, they'll be able to process the event a day later, then a few hours later, then even a few minutes later. The ultimate goal is for the client to develop internal and external self-awareness *as the event happens.*

Learning this art of being present means being able to recognize that you've made up stories about the other person in the exact moment when those false, internal scripts collide with your present reality. Practicing awareness means that you begin to see how the stories you tell yourself don't align with reality. With practice, the timeframe you'll require to see the conflict between your fictional narratives and real life should lessen, even to the point where you'll begin to disclose your fabrications to your significant other in order to assess whether or not you're actually listening to him or her.

> Learning this art of being present means being able to recognize that you've made up stories about the other person in the exact moment when those false, internal scripts collide with your present reality.

Awareness by itself is an abstract word, so let's break it down into three areas. Below is an adapted version of Rick Carson's (noted expert in Gestalt/Existential Therapy and a mentor of mine over the years) work on the three zones of awareness:

- Our BODIES

- Our MINDS

- Our EMOTIONS

> Being aware of our BODIES means noticing our physical reactions, like the tightening of the chest when you're stressed or the proverbial butterflies in your stomach if you're nervous.

> Being aware of our MINDS means noticing where our thoughts take us, whether to the past or to the future, as well as what those thoughts tell us about ourselves.

> **Being aware of our EMOTIONS means noticing our internal world and learning how to name our feelings.**

At any point in time, we can choose to be aware of none, all, or any of these zones. More often than not, we tend to gravitate toward one zone of awareness to the detriment of the others. The art of being present requires that we become adept and comfortable at living in all three zones of awareness. As I recommend in many of my suggested strategies for relational health, discovering balance is key.

PRACTICAL STEPS TOWARD HEIGHTENING YOUR AWARENESS

Learning to be present involves getting in touch with your senses, being aware of both your external and internal environments, grounding yourself, and learning how to guide your mind and emotions. These are all practical ways we can "show up" in our relationships so that an opportunity for true connection might occur. Let's look at each of these practices individually.

Exercise external awareness.

In order to engage another person in the here and now, you must learn to be aware of each one of your senses, from sight, sound, and touch to even smell and taste. Depending on the context of the situation, some senses may dominate others, but noticing that you're actually seeing, hearing, touching, smelling, or tasting something in particular in the present moment is a simple first step toward teaching yourself how to relate to someone else on a less superficial level. Increasing your external awareness demands that you take notice of the present.

Exercise internal awareness.

There's an additional type of awareness, more than being externally aware of your surroundings and how your environment affects your senses. You must also learn how to be internally aware. Another way to say this is that you must learn how to be mentally and emotionally present with another person. The body can only live in the present, but the mind has a tendency to live in the past, the present, or the future. More often than not, the mind wants to jump in a time machine and escape the present for the fond memories or regrets of the past or the hopes, dreams, or anxieties of the future. For this reason, practicing external awareness is often easier than practicing internal awareness. Learning how to be aware of what's going on within you is just as important as seeing what's affecting you from the outside.

> The body can only live in the present, but the mind has a tendency to live in the past, the present, or the future.

Additionally, you have the ability to change the way you think about something, which in turn can change your behavior. This is called neuroplasticity, a scientific word that means your mind has the ability to reorganize itself through the formation of new neural connections. We possess very little control over the initial thoughts that pop into our minds in any given situation, but we can choose how long we allow that initial thought to linger in our minds, as well as what thought can replace that initial thought. In other words, you have the power to change the way you think about another person. In the parlance of this book, the mind's neuroplasticity allows you to give up on the relationship in your head in order to focus on true connection with the real person in front of you, and much of this work begins with an internal awareness of your thoughts.

> **You have the power to change the way you think about another person.**

In a similar vein, reframing a person in your mind can help you approach the relationship from a different perspective. By coming at a troubling relationship from a different angle, you may be better able to digest the situation, thus decreasing your anxiety and helping to change your behavior as well as the way you approach the other person. Reframing is often best accomplished after the last step of the Auxano Approach© to communication and relationships: SEEK MORE INFORMATION.

Ground yourself.

If you have trouble focusing on the present and "showing up" in your relationships, literally place your feet on the ground. Take a seat and place both of your feet firmly on the ground as an outside reminder of an internal, intentional change of mind. With that purposeful movement, you're telling both your body and your mind to be grounded in the present.

Learning the art of being present requires that you see the deep and often unnoticed connection between your body and your mind. For instance, have you ever noticed your physical sensations when you're stressed? Your breathing may become shallow and quick and only escape through your nose, your tongue may go to the roof of your mouth, your jaw may clench, and your teeth may grind. If we can exercise external awareness and see when these physical signs happen to us, we can learn how to delve deeper and exercise internal awareness. That is, if we're short of breath, we can subsequently ask ourselves, "What's making me breathe like this? Why am I tense? What internal issue has me so worked up that it's affecting my breathing?" The more we become aware of these outer signs of our inward emotional states of being, the more we can learn how to be present with another person.

> **Learning the art of being present requires that you see the deep and often unnoticed connection between your body and your mind.**

Guide your mind and emotions.

Lastly, being present requires that we show our mind and emotions the way back to the present. Like I said before, the body can only exist in the present, but our minds love to escape to the past or the future. That's why we tell ourselves made-up stories based on our personal history or our hopes, dreams, and fears. When we allow our minds to dwell on the past, we focus on the "coulda, woulda, shouldas." That is, we think to ourselves, "I could have done that. I would have done this. I should have done that." Because we either don't want to face the present moment or because we want to exert control over the present moment, our minds go back in time as we ask ourselves what we could have done differently so that we wouldn't be experiencing the present circumstance. On the other hand, when we allow our minds to dream about the future, we focus on what-ifs. These what-if questions can be hopeful or fearful: "What if I get that promotion?" or "What if she dies?" However, whether your mind runs to the past or flies to the future, it's not existing in the present, causing you to miss out on truly connecting with another person.

> **Being present requires that we show our mind and emotions the way back to the present.**

When you notice your mind going somewhere else during a conversation, work to pull your mind back to the present. This can be accomplished by the simple act of re-establishing eye contact, then truly listening to what the other person is saying. In this moment, set aside your own agenda. If it helps, visualize yourself putting your own thoughts and feelings on a shelf for a while—not forever, but just while the other person is talking. Pay attention to what the person is saying and be genuinely interested in his or her words, thoughts, and feelings.

> **When you notice your mind going somewhere else during a conversation, work to pull your mind back to the present.**

Noticing your breathing is a good next step. If you're not breathing normally, it may be a sign that your mind is preoccupied. Repeating back to the other person what he or she just said can help your mind refocus on the conversation. As you become more adept at noticing when your mind wanders, you'll start to learn your own "tells," the things you do, say, or feel that cause you to live in the past or dream about the future instead of really connecting with another person.

Pause here and consider these questions:

- Do you try to make amends?

- How would you rate yourself on making significant connections with others?

- What most often gets in your way?

Think back to a recent one-on-one conversation. Did you actually "show up" emotionally and mentally for the conversation? Did you look the person in the eye, and listen—really listen—to what that person was saying? If these are areas where you have difficulty, practice the tips that I've mentioned during your next conversation. Yes, it may feel a little strange at first, but if you make it a habit for all of your relationships, you'll graduate from experiencing moments of being present to living a life of presence, the topic of the next chapter.

WHAT IT LOOKS LIKE TO PRACTICE BEING PRESENT

How does the art of being present look in real life? Let's go back to Steve and Lauren the day after her cancer diagnosis.

Although they had been seeing a counselor prior to her diagnosis, Steve was still somewhat stoic and withdrawn from Lauren. When the shift was forced upon them, he wrestled with how much he should share with his wife about his own fears. He was worried that she already had too much to handle as it was without adding his own fears to the mix. But Lauren was a few steps ahead in her desire to seek relational health with her spouse. With plenty of time to ponder what her counselor had said, she'd taken his suggestions to heart and wanted to start implementing them as soon as possible.

When Steve came home from work the day after her diagnosis, Lauren asked him to sit down across from her.

"Steve, I'd like us to have an honest conversation right now. I know it won't be easy, but we need to do this."

"Okay, hon. I'll try."

"I want to know how you're doing with everything we're going through right now," Lauren asks.

Steve's eyes wander around the room.

"Steve, can you look at me? I know you don't want to talk about this, but I need to know that you're here right now. I can't do this alone."

Steve glances at his wife and, in an instant, sees within his mind all the ways he's walled himself off from her over the years. He saw himself through her eyes, how he would always escape to the garage when he didn't want to talk about something difficult, jokingly put her down from time to time, and argue with her over trivial matters because his work life was stressful. In that moment, he felt shame for the stories he'd told himself about Lauren. In an effort to connect with his wife who truly needed him in this moment, he thought back to what their counselor had recommended.

Steve sat upright and consciously placed two feet on the floor. He took three deep breaths and allowed his gaze to meet his wife's. She smiled back at him, fully aware of what he was trying to do. Even though no words had passed between the two for a full minute, Lauren felt a deep love for her husband. She could tell that he was trying to overcome his past tendencies in order to honestly connect with her.

For the next two hours, they shared most everything they'd always been afraid to tell each other.

BECOMING A PERSON OF PRESENCE

"Your true home is in the here and the now." | Thích Nhất Hạnh

PRESENT VS. PRESENCE

The art of being present and becoming a person of presence may appear too similar at first glance, but important distinctions must be made between the two. To start with, being present often signifies a momentary state. Because of the many distractions in our lives, we have to do the hard work of truly being present in our relationships. We must learn how to reign in our wandering thoughts and emotions. In contrast, being a person of presence suggests that we've done that hard work and have effectively graduated to a heightened state of constant awareness in our relationships. Being a person of presence means that you've practiced being present with others for so long that it's become an ingrained habit, or a natural state of being where you don't have to consciously think about whether or not you're truly connecting with another person.

> **Being a person of presence suggests that we've done that hard work and have effectively graduated to a heightened state of constant awareness in our relationships.**

Learning to be present is like a child learning to crawl. It is a necessary and conscious effort that we must make in order to succeed at the next level. Becoming a person of presence is like walking. Once we've learned the proper techniques and have made them a daily habit, we never have to give conscious thought to exactly how we're doing what we're doing. In other words, you have to learn the art of being present before you can become a person of presence. To use a useful cliché, you have to crawl before you can walk.

When I'm talking with my clients, I often describe this difference between being present and being a person of presence as a continuum. The image of a continuum is a helpful way to visualize the series of steps that I'm recommending. In regards to elevating yourself from momentary acts of being present to living a life defined by presence, the continuum looks like this:

Continuum of Presence

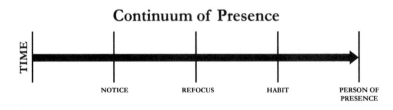

- I NOTICE and am aware that I'm not being fully present in my relationships.

- I see the need for being present and consciously work to REFOCUS my full attention on others.

- As being present with others becomes a daily HABIT, it takes less effort for me to honestly relate to another person.

- In becoming a PERSON OF PRESENCE, the possibility for true connection in all of my relationships greatly increases.

We've already discussed many ways in which you can tell whether or not you're being present in your relationships, from withdrawal to confrontation to a mind that always wants to live in a different time zone. A simple way to tell whether or not you're deeply connecting with another person is to take note of your experience of time. What do I mean by that? Consider the last time you felt like you had a truly meaningful conversation with someone else in your life. Do you feel as if you ran out of time, as if time actually sped up? More often than not, when we're truly engaging with another person, time flies. On the other hand, if you're distracted, disconnected, or unfocused, time appears to slow down. Sometimes all it takes is a glance at your watch to tell you whether or not you're being fully present.

In finally noticing our disconnect with others—i.e., defining many of the stories we tell ourselves as fabrications—we begin to see where our internal stories collide with reality and cause harm to our relationships. Consequently, we want to work to mend these relationships through practicing the art of being present. The more we do so, the more likely it is that we'll become people of presence. **The reason we want to become people of presence**

is that it greatly increases our chances for connection, and there is nothing our souls desire more than a meaningful connection with another person. Recall what I said in a previous chapter: we all desire to know and to be known.

Our human need for deep relationships was made readily apparent to me during an internship I held after graduating from graduate school/seminary. I worked as a chaplain for a hospital, where much of the time meant helping the dying and their loved ones properly grieve their mortality. I recall one woman in particular who approached me and began to earnestly question me as to why God would have allowed her husband to suffer in a coma for nine months following a terrible car accident. Even though I had years of schooling behind me, the moment itself caught me off guard. As a recent graduate, I didn't know what to say, and the woman quickly left the room. I had missed my moment to connect with her when she very much needed to connect with someone in order to make sense of her hurting world.

I didn't offer many answers because I didn't want to fall into the trap that so often happens to people of faith when it comes to death and grief. We use godly sounding platitudes to hide behind, like "He's in a better place now," or "God must have wanted her back." These sweet-sounding but ultimately empty words do little for the grieving while making us feel somewhat better.

I relayed the event to my supervisor, and she told me something deeply impacting: "It's critical that you focus on being a 'person of presence'." She admonished me to go back and spend focused time with the grieving wife, not necessarily answering her questions, but seeking to know her experience. She suggested using phrases like, "What's this experience been like for you?

For your kids?" She encouraged me to be present. For me, that meant being God's "hands and feet" to her by simply offering my presence and my time. What I learned during my internship is that offering my presence was the best gift I could give to those who were dying or grieving.

In a similar vein, a pastor friend of mine related the time he visited with a family who'd just lost their children in a car accident. He cried as soon as he saw the family, then mumbled and cried through a prayer for the family before leaving the house—after staying for just a few minutes. He recalls thinking that he was the worst pastor in the world for how he failed to handle the situation. Weeks later, the family sent him a letter saying how thankful they were for his visit and how well he handled the moment. Because he had simply offered his humanity and his presence in one of the world's most challenging situations, he deepened relational bonds with this grieving family.

Our inner selves crave connection like our outer selves crave food and water. Like Henri Young in *Murder in the First*, relational starvation can be just as deadly as physical starvation. In learning how to relate to the real people in your life and not just the made-up characters from the stories in your mind, you're preparing yourself as well as you can for the possibility of connection. While the other person may have their own issues to work on that prevent true connection from occurring, their refusal to meet you on even ground takes nothing away from you. In fact, it may even spur you on to continue exercising presence with that person in order to eventually get past the barriers that they've erected.

So, if you don't see a person of presence when you look in the mirror, how will you know that person when they do decide to show up? What does a person of presence look like?

SIX CHARACTERISTICS OF PRESENCE

While there are more than six defining qualities for a person of presence, the six skills that I am going to describe provide an effective template for assessing your own predilection for presence. Without these six particular traits manifesting themselves in your relationships with others, your ability to exercise true presence will be consistently thwarted. A person of presence lives out these attributes:

- Self-confidence

- Boundaries

- Openness

- Vulnerability

- Humility

- Self-awareness

When a person's inner life is firing on all six of these cylinders, their learned ability of presence provides the catalytic kick that unhealthy relationships often need. When both people in a relationship begin to act as people of presence, a true, deep, and lasting connection has a much higher percentage of occurring. Though cultivating these traits requires difficult, inner work, the goal is worth the cost.

A PERSON OF PRESENCE HAS SELF-CONFIDENCE

For an example, let's look into Steve and Lauren's marriage a few months after they had begun seeing their therapist/counselor.

> For as long as she could remember, Steve had always characterized many of Lauren's ideas as "ridiculous." He used the term so often that she had even begun to have a slight physical reaction the moment he started to say the word. Though Steve thought little about what it was like for his wife when he said that one particular word, its constant use throughout the many years of their marriage had eroded Lauren's emotional skin to where a raw, deep nerve was struck every time he spoke the word. In other words, Lauren had a difficult time not taking that particular criticism to heart every time Steve used it.

> Finally, after a few counseling sessions to help Lauren learn what it means to "stand on her own two feet" and stand up for herself, she calmly and bravely confronted Steve the moment after he said, "You're being ridiculous."

> "I want to invite you into my mind and emotions when you say, 'You're being ridiculous.' Over the years you've said that phrase, I haven't said anything, but I've been quietly struggling inside with it. What I tell myself is that Steve must think less of me. For years, I have put myself in a 'one-down' position in our relationship, based on your words, and I want to stop making myself "less than." A part of that journey for me is getting clear on what you mean when you say that I'm being ridiculous. But before I continue to convince myself that that's what

you really think, let me ask you right now, do you really think I'm ridiculous?"

Steve hesitates, surprised at his wife's new confidence, then quietly replies, "No, it's just that sometimes I think what you're saying is ridiculous, like it just doesn't make sense to me. Come to think of it, my parents used to use that phrase all the time."

Lauren replies, "I never knew your parents used that phrase while you were growing up. Thank you for letting me know that this is not about me as a person, but about what I say not adding up for you. That is huge for me."

Steve nods his head, unsure of what Lauren's about to say or do because this is relational ground that they've never walked on before.

"Thank you for being honest with me, Steve. Even though I'm not going to take 'being ridiculous' so personally anymore, it would mean a lot to me if you could drop that phrase from daily use. Is that such a ridiculous request?" Lauren asks with a slight grin.

"Of course not, Lauren, and I'm sorry that my flippant words have caused you so much trouble over the years. I never knew."

This simple story shows what self-confidence in a relationship can look like. For Lauren, it meant reaching out to her husband even though she could have received a negative response in return. By asserting her self-confidence during her discussion with Steve, she was able to maintain her composure regardless of his response. In being secure within her own skin, she's also able to finally hear Steve's honest reply. She even learns the origination of the phrase that she had come to hate so much, and it actually breeds compassion in her for her husband, as she rightly surmises that Steve must have grown up with a constant barrage of being told he was ridiculous.

Also, take notice of the specific language Lauren uses to communicate her thoughts and feelings back to her husband: "I want to invite you into my mind and emotions" and "What I tell myself . . . " Such simple sentences can be used in a wide variety of settings in order to help two people to truly communicate with each other. Through the use of such language, Lauren's effectively inviting Steve to listen to the story that she's been telling herself about him.

What Lauren had learned prior to her confronting her husband is something that all of us need to learn, and then need to be reminded about on a consistent basis. Our value is not based on what others think about us. Neither is it determined by our career, our finances, our possessions, our connections, or our popularity. You determine your value. This is the essence of self-confidence. You should hear the loudest shouts of praise in your own voice. Brené Brown says, "Talk to yourself like you would talk to someone you love." Although self-confidence can quickly turn into arrogance, the right amount of self-confidence can drastically alter your relationships for the better.

> **Our value is not based on what others think about us.**

In regards to a lack of self-confidence, you have a choice as to whether or not you develop loyalty to the opinion that you don't possess innate value. In other words, you can choose to press pause on the negative beliefs you may hold about yourself and replace those thoughts with positive beliefs. As you begin to hear and combat the "negative narrator" in your head, you will become more adept at recognizing when you're buying into that negative voice as well as how to replace those confidence-defeating thoughts. The better you become at catching and arresting your negative narrator and separating yourself from such toxic, critical beliefs and words, the greater degree of success you can have in replacing those thoughts with thoughts of value, worth, and dignity.

On a personal note, I believe spirituality plays a role in self-confidence as well. My bias that I have experienced through research and in my own life is that God values me as well as every other human person. I feel incredible personal worth when I truly, internally, emotionally experience God's deep love for me and for others. In fact, the Latin roots of the word "confidence"—*con* and *fide*—mean "with faith." In other words, whether I'm confident in myself or confident in God living in me—confidence requires faith.

A PERSON OF PRESENCE HAS BOUNDARIES

A different way to look at having self-confidence is known as setting proper boundaries. For instance, in the story above, if Lauren had chosen to share a bit more of her honest feelings with Steve, she may have said something like, "What you say to me in off-the-cuff remarks creates some sadness in me. It frustrates me too. But I'm not going to let it wound me." By verbally naming how she's been hurt in the past, but choosing not to let those words wound her going into the future, Lauren's setting up a healthy internal boundary in her relationship with Steve.

Author and therapist Pia Mellody describes boundary making in a helpful way. The following section comes from her seminal work on relationships, *Facing Codependency*, as well as an additional worksheet associated with that book.

Boundary systems are invisible and symbolic 'fences' that have three purposes:

- To keep people from coming into our space and abusing us.

- To keep us from going into the space of others and abusing them.

- To give each of us a way to embody our sense of 'who we are.'

Boundary systems have two parts: external and internal.

> **Our EXTERNAL boundary allows us to choose our distance from other people and enables us to give or refuse permission for them to touch us . . .**

> **Our INTERNAL boundary protects our thinking, feelings, and behavior and keeps them functional.**

When we are using our internal boundary, we can take responsibility for our thinking, feelings, and behavior and keep them separate from that of others, and stop blaming them for what we think, feel, and do. Our internal boundary also allows us to stop taking responsibility for the thoughts, feelings, and behaviors of others, allowing us to stop manipulating and controlling those around us.

I visualize my external boundary as a bell-shaped jar that fits over me. Its surfaces move out or in as I control distance or touch with others. I visualize my internal boundary as a bullet-proof vest with small doors that open only toward the inside. I am in control of whether they open or are kept shut.

> **I visualize my external boundary as a bell-shaped jar that fits over me.**

> **I visualize my internal boundary as a bullet-proof vest with small doors that open only toward the inside.**

In a section entitled "Setting Functional Boundaries," Mellody continues:

External Physical Boundary

You create the 'self protective' part of your external boundary when someone is approaching you. You do this by determining how close you allow the person to stand to you and whether or not you are going to allow him or her to touch you.

You create the 'other protective' part of your external physical boundary when you are physically approaching another person. You do this by being respectful of an eighteen-inch social distance between you and the other person and by not touching him or her without his or her permission. . . .

Internal Boundary

You establish the 'self protective' part of your internal boundary when someone is talking. First, set your personal boundary. Then, say to yourself that the other person is responsible for creating what he or she is saying. You only take into yourself what is the truth for you. Block the rest by following this procedure:

- If it is true, let the information in, embrace it, and allow yourself to have feelings about it.

- If you determine that the information is not true, allow it to bounce off your boundary.

- If the data is questionable, gather data regarding the information.

As you observe and analyze the information, you can determine if the information is 'true' or 'not true.' If it is true, filter the information and have feelings about it. If the information is not true, block it and remove it from your boundary.

- True: Filter/Filter & Feel

- Not True: Block/Block

- Questionable: Filter/Block & Gather Data

You establish the 'other protective' part of your internal boundary when you are verbally sharing yourself. As you share your thoughts and feelings, you say to yourself, 'I have created what I am saying and feeling. I am the only one responsible for my thoughts and feelings.'

These are powerful words from Pia. A friend and colleague, Charles Vorkoper, once told me that relationships are 98% about boundaries. Boundaries exist to protect relationships and to protect us individually. When we try to change and control someone else's behavior, that violates our own boundaries first and foremost. By being proactive about both the external and internal boundaries we set within ourselves and for our relationships, we're working toward becoming people of presence.

> **Relationships are 98% about boundaries.**

A PERSON OF PRESENCE HAS OPENNESS

When my wife and I openly communicate with each other (i.e., when we are at our best and functioning like mature adults), and we fear that we're missing pertinent information, we will interject a number of phrases into our conversation to ensure that we're understanding each other. We will use phrases like:

"What I heard was . . . Is that what you meant?"

"The story I'm telling myself right now is . . . Is that true?"

"What I'm making up in my mind is . . . Is that on target?"

We may also ask pointed questions about how we might be feeling, like whether we are angry, sad, or hurt.

In my marriage, I try to avoid being the therapist/counselor in order to actually be in the relationship with my wife. When I am successful, I ask these types of questions to ensure that I'm not basing my feelings and behaviors off faulty information. If I make up incorrect beliefs about my wife which turn into wrong actions on my part, I lead us down a path of anger, hurt, and distance in our relationship. What is 'crazy-making' on my part is that the disconnect in our relationship at that moment is the result of some small issue that likely wasn't even true. As you can see, I am still working to strengthen my relational muscle in my life and marriage. This is why learning how to seek new information when you're bereft of facts is such an important part of presence.

A phrase I often use with my clients is **posture curiosity.** That means being willing to ask relevant questions in order to seek the truth about a situation. Sometimes asking such questions can be hard because the answers you receive could hurt you. Oftentimes we don't want to seek more information because we're already content with the story in our heads. But, like I said before, modeling openness and posturing curiosity can prevent you from filling in the blanks of your relationships with false information and made-up fantasies.

But relationships involve two people. So in addition to being open to new information from the other person, learning how to communicate your own wants and needs in a mature and adult way is important. This can be accomplished by receiving

THE STORIES WE TELL OURSELVES

the other person's information without judging them or taking their thoughts personally (i.e., good internal boundaries) while simultaneously standing up for yourself.

It's at this point that you may begin to see how the six characteristics of a person of presence influence each other. Without self-confidence and proper boundary setting, a person who chooses to exercise openness may feel deeply judged when seeking new information. They may take the other person's word as the whole truth about themselves, essentially allowing the other person's story to dictate their own self-worth. That's why a person of presence must learn how to live out these characteristics in synchronization and not just pick and choose which ones seem most appealing.

A PERSON OF PRESENCE HAS VULNERABILITY

In Brené Brown's book, *Daring Greatly,* she says, "Vulnerability is the birthplace of love, belonging, joy, courage, empathy, and creativity. It is the source of hope, empathy, accountability, and authenticity. If we want greater clarity in our purpose or deeper and more meaningful spiritual lives, vulnerability is the path."

To be vulnerable requires that we tear down our self-constructed barriers. It means that we dismantle the false stories we've been telling ourselves, the ones we use over and over in order to protect ourselves from being hurt again. To be vulnerable means that we're capable of communicating our wants and needs in a mature, adult way. It takes vulnerability to "stand on our own two feet" and say what we really feel. It takes "daring greatly" to let yourself possibly be hurt again.

> **To be vulnerable requires that we tear down our self-constructed barriers.**

When we lack an ability to be vulnerable, we inhibit relational growth. When we fail to truly communicate our feelings, we run the risk of the other person running roughshod over our lives. Without revealing the stories we're telling ourselves about someone else, the stories they're telling themselves may dominate the relationship. It's only when both people in a relationship can learn to trust each other and exercise vulnerability on a deep basis can a true relational connection occur. People of presence practice being vulnerable, yet with healthy boundaries and self-esteem.

> **Without revealing the stories we're telling ourselves about someone else, the stories they're telling themselves may dominate the relationship.**

It's interesting to me, especially in light of the major theme of this book, that Brené Brown speaks about our stories in relationship to learning to be vulnerable: "Owning our story can be hard but not nearly as difficult as spending our lives running from it. Embracing our vulnerabilities is risky but not nearly as dangerous as giving up on love and belonging and joy—the experiences that make us the most vulnerable. Only when we are brave enough to explore the darkness will we discover the infinite power of our light." In other words, becoming a person of presence is not an easy task. It requires soul-searching that could reveal negative personality traits, pent-up emotions, or difficult-to-face issues stemming from the past. But the reward of deep relational connection is worth the risk we take in becoming vulnerable, both with others and with ourselves.

In learning how to come to terms with our own insecurities and how they sometimes derail our relationships, we will start to see the light: that true and deep connection our souls long to experience.

A PERSON OF PRESENCE HAS HUMILITY

Someone who's learned to be fully present with another person must be humble. Humility doesn't mean making yourself "less than" the other person or constantly bending to their demands, feelings, or actions. Rather, it means being able to admit when you're wrong and taking ownership of your own behavior. Part of learning to stand on your own two feet means that, in addition to asserting your own thoughts and feelings, you also have to own up to where you fall short in the relationship.

Take a moment and answer these questions. When you hurt another person:

- Do you try to make amends?

- When you realize that you've wronged someone else, are you proactive about healing the relationship? Or do you consistently maintain that your opinion is always the right opinion?

- Do you allow the practices of openness and information finding to truly influence your decisions, feelings, and actions? In other words, if you're honestly listening to another person and not just to the story in your head, do you take their thoughts and feelings into account?

- Do their words ever change your thoughts? Or, do you casually dismiss them because you have better ideas?

A person of presence doesn't practice humility out of deference to the other person, but out of deference to the relationship. If such a person acts humble for the other person's benefit, it may lead to a "one-down" relationship where one person consciously makes themselves "less than" the other person. This could occur for a host of reasons. On the other hand, when someone humbles themselves in deference to the relationship itself, this allows for the two people to meet each other as equals. Because the person of presence can admit when they're wrong—notice that this requires vulnerability—the other person is much more likely to trust them with their own true thoughts and feelings.

> **Humility doesn't mean making yourself "less than" the other person or constantly bending to their demands, feelings, or actions. Rather, it means being able to admit when you're wrong and taking ownership of your own behavior.**

A PERSON OF PRESENCE HAS SELF-AWARENESS

As I have mentioned, self-awareness is an integral part of the entire process of learning to become a person of presence. Over time, you begin to learn what your particular triggers are, that is, the words and actions of others that have the capability of upsetting your internal balance. As you become more and more self-aware, you can learn specific ways to combat those automatic reactions so that they don't have an opportunity to hurt your relationships.

For instance, a self-aware person of presence will allow themselves to emotionally react to certain situations, but then react to that reaction with a proven strategy to calm themselves *in the moment*. If you'll recall, we covered these particular anxiety-lessening strategies in a previous chapter. Because such emotional reactions are impossible to prevent, we must learn coping strategies to help us effectively process our thoughts and feelings in our relationships. By allowing ourselves to be emotionally reactive, we exhibit vulnerability, but by counteracting our negative emotions with calming techniques, we can lessen the relational damage our initial emotions may cause.

When we practice present self-awareness, we can view ourselves on a continuum of "one-up" or "one-down" relationships. We don't have to react to another person in anger because we're not seeking to manipulate them or make them feel "less than" so that they'll do what we want. Neither do we have to react to another person with grave respect or heightened kindness because we want them to accept us or come around to our way of thinking. **We want to exist in the middle of that continuum where we meet another person as equals, allowing our emotions to exist, but not allowing them to have complete sway over the relationship.** It is important to seek to live in the balance between our emotional selves and our rational minds. A person of presence can do this *in the moment*, constantly evaluating whether or not one side of themselves is acting as a dictator over their relationships.

ARE YOU A PERSON OF PRESENCE?

One by one, consider the six characteristics of presence I've outlined and whether or not you see evidence of these factors in your relationships:

Do you have self-confidence in your relationships?

Are you able to stand up for yourself, your ideas, and your feelings? Can you say what you mean, even if what you say may be hurtful to another person? What's one way you can begin to practice self-confidence?

Do you have proper and healthy boundaries in your relationships?

Looking back at Pia Mellody's definitions, how would you describe your internal boundaries? Your external boundaries? With which people in your life do you have unhealthy boundaries? What can you do now to change that?

How open are you to new information?

How often do you ask follow-up questions in order to seek further information, especially in difficult circumstances or when you may have already made up your mind about the matter?

How vulnerable do you allow yourself to be in relationships?

How much of what you think actually finds its release through your words and actions in regards to other people? What barriers have you constructed that prevent you from being vulnerable? What do you fear by being vulnerable with someone else?

Do you practice humility? One of the best ways to assess this is to consider the last time you verbally told another person, "I'm sorry and I was wrong because . . . " Is there someone you need to say that to soon?

Lastly, are you aware of the ways that your emotions may take over your relationships?

In a broader sense, are you aware of each of these issues *in the moment* of your relationships? As the last chapter attested, we can learn the art of being present and reap the benefits of such practice, but it's not until these characteristics reside in the muscle memory of our minds that we can become people of presence.

THE STORY WE (NOW) TELL OURSELVES

"BREATHE. Breathe in and breathe deeply. Be PRESENT. Do not be past. Do not be future. Be now." | Kyle Lake

Pause here.

Take a deep breath.

Consider what you've read in this book.

Does it resonate with you? Are you now more aware of the stories you tell yourself? Do you see how those stories may have been negatively affecting your relationships and increasing your anxiety? Have you discovered the origin of the stories you tell yourself? Do you feel better equipped to silence those stories in order to connect on a deeper level with the people in your life? Have you begun to practice the art of being present so that you might become a person of presence?

When you press pause on your assumptions and avoid jumping to conclusions in your relationships, you will enjoy a higher quality of life, one marked by fulfilling relationships and less anxiety. The journey to that point will likely be challenging and may be filled with awkward moments as you learn to be present more often and more fully, but the rewards of following this path are worth the effort.

> **When you press pause on your assumptions and avoid jumping to conclusions in your relationships, you will enjoy a higher quality of life, one marked by fulfilling relationships and less anxiety.**

Much of this journey requires you to do specific kinds of internal work in your own life, if you haven't already begun to do so. Learning to lessen the stories you tell yourself means you must discover the influential people and factors in your life.

Have you spent time with a professional, or in conversation with friends, to unearth the sometimes deeply buried scripts you use on a consistent basis to fill in the gaps of your relationship problems?

Have you considered how mass media like movies, TV, and the Internet work their influence into your stories?

Have you researched your family history, or observed your immediate family, to learn what family of origin issues may be influencing your stories?

Have you taken a loving but critical look at yourself, essentially stepping outside of yourself to see you for who you really are?

Have you considered how your own personal trauma, losses, past pain, or hurts may have held you back in your life?

Pause here and take a few minutes to consider what your own personal next steps may be in regard to the questions above.

EMOTIONAL AND RELATIONAL INTELLIGENCE

The Stories We Tell Ourselves has aimed to guide you down a pathway to emotional and relational maturity. All of the steps and strategies I've outlined along the way were for one dual purpose: to increase your emotional and relational intelligence.

In *Handle with Care*, the authors define emotional intelligence as "a way of recognizing, understanding, and choosing how we think, feel, and act. It shapes our interactions with others and our understanding of ourselves. It defines how and what we learn; it allows us to set priorities; it determines the majority of our daily actions. Research suggests it is responsible for as much as 80% of the 'success' in our lives."

To become emotionally intelligent requires a few things: we must first become aware of the fact that we tell ourselves stories, then we must notice what stories we tell ourselves, then we must discover these stories' origins. When we come to better understand ourselves—and that includes our stories, emotions, reactions, motivations, and a whole host of other influential factors in our lives—we gain emotional intelligence that allows more space in our lives for healthy relationships. However, becoming emotionally intelligence is an on-going process. There's no graduation. We must maintain a constant vigilance when it comes to noticing and acknowledging our human inclination toward self-centeredness and self-protection. Yet, such a continual, internal self-assessment increases our emotional intelligence, which necessarily leads to increased relational intelligence.

Relational intelligence is the ability to engage with others personally and professionally, as well as being able to manage yourself in relationships. Engaging with others includes displaying social skills, listening, working on healthy communication, and improving your ability to work within a team, and being able to empathize. Managing self includes noticing and being aware of your emotions in the moment, being able to manage your emotions under pressure, and choosing to transform negative thoughts or situations into positive ones.

When you strengthen your relational intelligence, you'll begin to notice much of what we've already discussed. You'll be able to manage your anxiety. You may begin to realize in real time that, in many situations, your anxiety is a choice and not something predicated upon another person or the present circumstance. You'll start to see how your stress affects your relationships, but you'll also know ways to prevent such stress from negatively influencing your relationships. You'll be able to become vulnerable with other people and even invite them to hear the story you're telling yourself about them. You'll be able to share your feelings more fluidly and fearlessly. You'll become bold in seeking information for the betterment of the relationship instead of relying on your mental vault of long-stored scripts. As you become more adept at being present with people, you'll become a person of presence, someone who doesn't have to work as hard or as often in order to stay focused when communicating.

With increased emotional intelligence comes decreased anxiety. With increased relational intelligence comes more fulfilling relationships. Together, this is a powerful equation for better living.

THE END OF MY STORY AND THE BEGINNING OF YOURS

Imagine what your life would be like with less stress and anxiety.

Imagine what your relationships would be like if they were deeper, longer-lasting, and more fulfilling.

Imagine what you would be like if the best possible version of you showed up to every one of your relationships.

For forty days, try the steps and strategies outlined in *The Stories We Tell Ourselves*.

See if what you imagined at the outset of this book might not become more than just a story I've told you.

See if it might, in fact, become your new reality.

DISCUSSION QUESTIONS

CHAPTER 1:
A STORY ABOUT OUR STORIES

1. Do you relate more to Steve, Lauren, or Emma in the opening story? Why?

2. Can you see how your mind makes up stories about others? In the past week, what is one story that you told yourself without having all of the information?

3. In which relationships do you tell yourself stories most often? With your spouse? Your children? A boss, coworker, or employee? A friend?

CHAPTER 2:
CLIENT STORIES

Do you identify yourself as any person in any of these stories: The $300,000 Mistake, Flirtation or Friendship, The Absent Alcoholic, Mom v. Dad, God of Judgment, Why?

Where do you think the stories we tell ourselves come from?

CHAPTER 3:
WHERE STORIES RUSH IN

What stories do you often tell yourself when stressed, either related to your partner, friend or professional relationships?

When it comes to looking at the anxiety, fact, and presence "gauges" of your mind, which one do you need to pay more attention to?

How have the stories you tell yourself negatively affected your relationships? Write down three examples.

CHAPTER 4:
ALL TOGETHER, ALL ALONE

When was the last time you felt lonely?

Do you employ defensive behavior (withdrawal, talking in circles, arguing, etc.) when asked about a touchy subject? Describe your typical reaction:

Do you have thoughts and/or behaviors which contribute to isolating you from others?

CHAPTER 5:
SEEKING SAFETY

What do you run to in order to feel safe? Do you seek safety in a relationship, at work, through money, with material possessions, or through some other means?

What belief about another person has ended up being a story that was not grounded in reality?

Do you sometimes try to control others? If so, what behavior do you practice as a means to control? Manipulation, criticism, avoidance, passive-aggression?

CHAPTER 6:
FAMILY TALES

What's the earliest memory you have of learning something from your primary caregiver, whether they said it or modeled it for you?

What are three basic ways that you grew up differently from your significant other?

Have those family of origin stories caused stress in your committed relationship? If so, in what ways?

What is one thing that your primary caregiver did or did not do that helped you grow and mature?

What is one thing that your primary caregiver did or did not do that held you back in your development?

What was it like to live with your mother? Your father? Your sibling(s)? In which parts of your life do you see yourself replicating their words or actions?

CHAPTER 7:
STORIES IN THE DARK

Do you believe that culture at large influences your behavior? Why or why not?

What are your favorite movies? Do they have similar themes? Can you identify areas in your life where the stories you told yourself were created with material from those movies?

How has your love life been impacted by movies, mass media, etc.?

CHAPTER 8:
THE PAIN OF THE PAST

Have you experienced a "personal earthquake," where it felt like the ground gave way beneath your feet and your world seemed to drastically change in a moment? Describe that experience and your initial reaction:

What are your "invisible scars" that few, if any, people know about?

How have painful experiences from your past contributed to the stories you tell yourself about other people?

How have you processed your past pain? Through professional counseling? Speaking with a friend? Journaling?

DISCUSSION QUESTIONS

CHAPTER 9:
SHIFT HAPPENS

Have you experienced a "shift" in your life? If so, what happened and how did it alter your relationships?

Can you recall a time where what you thought was true about someone else turned out to be false? How did your beliefs and opinions about the other person change the way you treated them?

What can you do to be proactive in restoring health to relationships that need your attention?

CHAPTER 10:
RELATIONSHIPS CAUSE STRESS

What relationships are currently causing stress in your life?

Do you expect conflict in your relationships? Why or why not?

In the last few years, how have you "acted in" or "acted out" when you've been stressed?

CHAPTER 11:
TOWARD LESS PERSONAL ANXIETY

Imagine what your life would look like with less stress and anxiety. How would it be different? Would you make different decisions?

How do you seek to control others? What relationships in your life do you try to control?

When stressed, what do you normally do?

CHAPTER 12:
TOWARD BETTER RELATIONSHIPS IN
MARRIAGE, FREINDSHIPS, AND BUSINESS

On a scale of 1 to 10, with 1 being "poor" and 10 being "excellent," rank your general contentment with your relationships in:

Marriage:

Friendships:

Business:

What have you done in the past to try to strengthen your relationships?

What was the result of your efforts in repairing broken relationships or enhancing dormant relationships?

How do you typically behave, in relationships, when you are stressed?

Describe your internal experience from the last stressful encounter you had with another person.

Describe your external experience from the last stressful encounter you had with another person.

When is the last time you told yourself a story about another person and it turned out to be true? What were the story, the reality, and your reaction to learning that you knew the truth about the situation? Did your correct guess change how you interacted with that person? If so, how?

When is the last time you discovered that someone else was telling themselves a story about you that wasn't true? What was the story and the reality, and how did that person treat you differently because of their story? How did you treat them after discovering their fabrication about you?

When the stories we tell ourselves turn out to be true, or when the stories others tell themselves about us turn out to be false, what steps should we take in order to seek or maintain relational wellness?

CHAPTER 13:
TOWARD MORE CONNECTION AND FULFILLMENT

Describe your general thoughts and feelings when your most important relationships seem disconnected and unfulfilling.

When an important relationship turns stressful, what do you typically do to try to salvage the relationship?

On a scale of 1 to 10, with 1 being "never" and 10 being "all the time," how often do you seek more information about a troubling situation? Why is that?

Recall the last time you were vulnerable and transparent and chose to share your feelings and the stories you tell yourself with another person. What happened immediately after that discussion? What was the relationship like a week later? A month later? A year later?

Do you allow for a "sliver of space" in your relationships? Why or why not?

Describe the last time you "stood on your own two feet." How did that make you feel? How did the other person react to you? Did the experience make you want to assert yourself again, or withdraw?

In what relationships could you immediately apply the Auxano Approach© to Communication?

CHAPTER 14:
THE ART OF BEING PRESENT

When is the last time you made direct, prolonged eye contact with someone? With someone who caused you to feel stressed? Why do many people refrain from such eye contact?

With how many people in your life do you feel a true connection?

Recall a recent, meaningful conversation you had with an important relationship. Describe your internal and external experience of that conversation.

Where do you lie on the Continuum of Awareness? Are you aware of your internal and external experience of a stress-inducing event a few years later, a few months later, a few days later, a few hours later, or during the moment that it's occurring?

What can you do to increase your awareness and become a "present artist?"

CHAPTER 15:
BECOMING A PERSON OF PRESENCE

What's the difference between being present and being a person of presence?

What's the benefit of becoming a person of presence?

Describe the last time you recall being fully present in a moment.

Of the six characteristics of presence (self-confidence, boundaries, openness, vulnerability, humility, and self-awareness), at which ones do you excel? Which ones do you need to work on?

How can you begin to practically implement each of those six characteristics into your relationships?

Do you "talk to yourself like you would to someone you love?" Why or why not? How does this affect your relationships?

What do your relational boundaries look like?

How do you "posture curiosity" in your relationships?

Describe the last time you were vulnerable with another person. How did they react? How did you react to their reaction?

When is the last time you "owned up" to a relationship mistake? Did you exercise humility in an attempt to repair the relationship? Why or why not?

CHAPTER 16:
THE STORY WE (NOW) TELL OURSELVES

Based on the strategies in this book, what can you do today to work toward better relationships in your life?

What stories have you been telling yourself about others that you need to press pause on?

On a scale of 1 to 10, with 1 being "very low" to 10 being "very high," rate your emotional intelligence. Why did you grade yourself that way?

Describe what you think your life could look like in a year if you had less stress and anxiety.

Describe what you think your life could look like in a year if you had deeper and more fulfilling relationships.

Describe what you think your life could look like in a year if the best possible version of you showed up to every one of your relationships?

ABOUT THE AUTHOR

R. Scott Gornto is a therapist, speaker, and author based in Dallas, Texas. Licensed by the State of Texas as a marriage and family therapist (LMFT), he is the founder and owner of Auxano Counseling and the creator of the *Auxano Approach*© to relationships. Scott also developed the *Truth About Marriage*® Workshop which assists couples in cultivating friendship, deepening intimacy, and improving partnership. He also created the *RQ Relational Intelligence* program for C-level executives and leaders.

Scott graduated from Baylor University (BA) and Fuller Theological Seminary (MDIV). He is also a graduate of the clinical residency program in pastoral counseling and psychotherapy from the Pastoral Counseling and Education Center (PCEC) in Dallas. He is a certified sex therapist (CST) with the American Association of Sexuality Educators, Counselors and Therapists (AASECT). He is a clinical member of the American Association of Marriage and Family Therapy (AAMFT), board certified supervisor by the Texas State Board of Examiners of Marriage and Family Therapists (TMFT) and the former President of the Dallas Association of Marriage and Family Therapy (DAMFT). He also serves on the advisory board for the Southern Methodist University (SMU) Program of Counseling.

He is an abstract artist (gorntoart.com) and enjoys golf, tennis, scuba diving and spending time with his wife, Crystal, and their two boys.

CONNECT ONLINE:
rscottgornto.com
info@rscottgornto.com
twitter.com/gornto
facebook.com/rscottgornto

INDEX